19th

Happy Birthday Jiggs. ' March :

I hope you enjoy pleasant memory's

Rusty & Ian

P.S: Don't give this away to anyone.

BY THE EL

Third Avenue and
its El at mid-century

by
Lawrence Stelter

Photography by
Lothar Stelter

**foreword: Joe Cunningham
introductions: Joe Franklin and
Stan Fischler
supplemental photos: Robert
Presbrey and Lawrence Stelter
design & layout: John Henderson
automotive resource: Ross Klein**

H&M PRODUCTIONS

(front cover) Family life thrives in mid-century New York in the shadow of the Empire State Building and the El. A 1950 Pontiac is parked on 3rd Avenue near the corner of 29th Street.

(title page) On a hazy summer morning, a northbound local pulls into 59th Street station. The Chrysler Building dominates the skyline. Joe's Restaurant was one of two Joe's landmarks. There was one on Court Street in Brooklyn and this one which was well renowned as a superior seafood place. A 1953 Oldsmobile turns on to 58th Street, while Ford and Willys trucks make deliveries on 3rd Avenue. A rare International Carryall negotiates 3rd Avenue beneath the El.

TECHNICAL NOTES

The photographs taken by Lothar Stelter in this book were taken with these cameras:
- **Contessa** (by Zeiss-Ikon) with a 45mm lens.
- **Rolliflex "Automat,"** a 120 film size camera with 35mm capability. Most of the close-ups of the windows were taken with this camera.
- **Leica IIIf** (by E. Leitz) with 50mm and 90mm lenses. 35mm and 135mm lenses by Canon were also used with this camera.

The films he used in both 35mm and 120 sizes were:
- **Kodachrome** (ASA film speed 10)
- **Kodachrome Type A** with a conversion filter produced many nighttime views.
- **Anscochrome** (ASA film speed 12)
- **Ektachrome** (ASA film speed 32)

Publishers note: All photographs that appear in this book were taken by Lothar Stelter unless otherwise indicated.

H&M PRODUCTIONS
193-07 45 AVE.
FLUSHING, NY 11358

ISBN 1-882608-12-7

PRESAGE

"....The old elevated railway is passing, just, as the old horse car passed. But it will live again whenever some youngster's imagination is stirred by a picture in a book or words of reminiscence of an old-timer. Then the rickety elevated train will roll again, the station platforms will tremble and the coals will be relit in the pot-bellied stoves......"

New York Times editorial
August 23, 1951

(left) Sign of a bygone age. A man repairing the street made of Belgian paving blocks. They were once the rule for Manhattan streets. This work is being done near 128th Street. Note the El is in the background.

LOTHAR STELTER

During the Autumn of 1950, Lothar Stelter of the Bronx started working for the New York Telephone Company. At age 19 he needed a means to support himself and his widowed mother. His first work assignment was as a cable splicer's helper along 3rd Avenue in Manhattan. He later advanced to a cable placer. Photography had always been an interest of his and a friend introduced him to 35 millimeter color slides. During the Summer of 1951, Mr. Stelter purchased a Contessa camera and soon began recording scenes up and down 3rd Avenue. Oftentimes the superintendents of the buildings where he was assigned allowed him to record the views from the roofs. Lunch time and before or after work found him composing the scenes you have before you; moments frozen in time...

(left) Lothar Stelter, in 1953, at the 76th Street station

JOSEPHINE STELTER

TABLE OF CONTENTS

PRESAGE..03
LOTHAR STELTER, PHOTOGRAPHER..03
FOREWORD..05
INTRODUCTIONS...06
ACKNOWLEDGEMENTS...07
DEDICATION..07
PREFACE...07
MANHATTAN MAP...08
BRIEF HISTORY OF MANHATTAN ELS..09
CHAPTER ONE: THE THIRD AVENUE EL AS AN EDIFICE....................10
     STATIONS AND STAINED GLASS.................................10
     STRUCTURE...20
     THE 'EL' AND THE SNOW..22
     EN ROUTE THE 'EL'..30
     PASSENGERS...30
     ROLLING STOCK...32
     THE REAR DOOR..33
CHAPTER TWO: A TRIP UP THIRD AVE...34
     NEIGHBORHOODS & LANDMARKS...............................34
          CHINATOWN...35
          THE BOWERY–LOWER EASTSIDE............36
          COOPER SQ.–LOWER EAST SIDE.............40
          GRAMERCY PARK–BELLEVUE..................45
          MURRAY HILL–KIPS BAY.........................48
          MIDTOWN–TURTLE BAY.........................55
          LENOX HILL...76
          YORKVILLE..82
          EAST HARLEM.......................................95
     THE END..108
CHAPTER THREE: EPILOG...116
     REMNANTS..117
     A TRIP UP TODAY'S THIRD AVENUE.............................118
BIBLIOGRAPHY..123
CHARLES ADDAMS CARTOON..124

FOREWORD

In January 1994, I was interviewed by Brian Lehrer, the host of the WNYC-AM radio talk show "On the Line." The subject was the history of New York's rapid transit in regard to the re-release of a book which I had co-authored with Leonard DeHart. During the interview, I mentioned that I believe that many of the city's elevated lines were demolished prematurely. I was contacted subsequently by a Mr. Lawrence Stelter, who sent me a paper which he had authored. In it, he documented some of the statistics, issues and political interests which lay behind the alleged "public improvement" (as the demolitions were called.) We met sometime later, and he mentioned that he hoped to publish an extensive collection of color pictures which his father had taken in vicinity of the 3rd Avenue El.

My attitude was ambivalent at best. On the one hand, I have heard so often about a treasure trove of "unbelievable" items, only to find the material is duplicative at best. On the other hand, I was intrigued for I just missed the El.; I was fortunate in having seen much of the character of Yorkville and surrounding areas before the old areas were swept away in the name of "redevelopment." After a delay of two months, I made an appointment to see the photos, but I did so without any great anticipation.

I was never more wrong. From the very first scene I was pulled to the screen. The character, the color, the sense of immediacy was overwhelming. There was a sense of time frozen; were I to look away for but a moment, one of the people or a dog, or perhaps an auto or an El car would betray a subtle movement. When we took a break, someone inquired as to what I thought.

The only response which I could offer was that I felt compelled to jump into the picture. And that compulsion is powerful, indeed. Long gone *Herald-Tribunes* and *Saturday Evening Posts* beckon from a plethora of newsstands tucked beneath El stairways. The scent of steak and potatoes seems to waft from a dozen eating places. Movie theaters offer cool respite and first run classics such as "On the Waterfront." My later, more sober reaction was: You've got to get this out there to all the people who experienced it. For those who missed it, the photos are a doorway to the recent past.

After the passage of some time, here it is. Open the pages and step into a world you may remember. Perhaps you never knew it. No matter, for you can wander amid the individual lives and daily commerce of decades ago. Meet folks who were born in the nineteenth century but are still middle-aged. Feel the warmth of the sun and a cool river breeze as you stand upon the wooden El platform at a tranquil moment. Feel the vibration of the approaching train and smell the aged, dusty wood. Taste cold snowflakes as they fall from a leaden sky. Smile at a proud dad and grandad as they take a small boy for a morning stroll. Watch as a pretty young woman checks her hair in the reflection of Victorian glasswork. It is all here, along with much more. There is enough to please the most critical of iconoclasts. So step through the pages to another time; a time when lively people in thriving communities lived, worked and played by the El!

Joe Cunningham

INTRODUCTIONS

BILL MARK

When Lawrence Stelter first called me about a book on the 3rd Avenue El., I said right away it would be a "good topic." I know that might sound self-serving from the King of Nostalgia, yet you will find that the photos in this book will become your ticket back to those wonderful days. Seldom have I seen a collection of images that is so comprehensive and realistic. It brought back the old days for me as it will for many of you. It must have been down on the Bowery where the train ran so close to the houses that I thought I was in people's living rooms. You could really see both the insides of New Yorkers' lives and the "outside" city from the El! Too bad, the subway does not compare nor does a bus ride today.

Unlike Martin Block's radio show which I hosted, "The Make-Believe Ballroom," this book is not make-believe. Those of us who were there went to the musicals announced from the movie marquees. "Hey there, you with the stars in your eyes...." played from the radio and was hummed by the people in these pictures. The new TV antennas received the Ed Sullivan Show and "The Honeymooners." Meanwhile, enjoy this publication thoroughly and maybe, as you peruse its pages, we will meet again on or by the El!

Joe Franklin

There were Els and there were Els; but there was only one elevated line that really mattered, and that was The Third Avenue El.

Take it from one who rode them all.

Brooklynite by birth, I had the good fortune to regularly ride the Myrtle Avenue El (practically in my backyard), Lexington Avenue El (Brooklyn's first); not to mention The Culver Line, Canarsie Line and, of course, the wonderful Broadway (Brooklyn) route to Jamaica.

Each and every one of them had their virtues but, alas, none of them was what you would call a signature El.

That category was reserved for the Third Avenue El for many reasons; not the least of which was that it traversed Manhattan's spine. It coupled Wall Street with Yorkville; it skirted the Empire State and Chrysler skyscrapers and, of course, it soared over The Bowery.

If they had charged five bucks a ride it would have been a bargain just for the scenery alone. And that, by the way, explains why many of the wonderful photos here depict riders simply looking at the fascinating cavalcade of people and things around them.

The Third Avenue El was as much New York as Times Square, Columbus Circle, Central Park and The Battery. And for a train buff like me, it was as fun to ride as ever I enjoyed; especially when I was lucky enough to sprint down the center track with an express.

Fortunately, some Els still remain within New York City in parts of Brooklyn and for a very short spin over Broadway between 122nd and 130th Streets in Manhattan.

Unfortunately, the one El that really mattered is no longer with us.

Sacrificed to that ole debbil "progress," The Third Avenue El went down just as I finished college; and, if I learned anything from that experience, it was that it didn't have to go and shouldn't have been eliminated.

But that's old business.

The new business, namely this utterly wonderful book that captures the essence of the Third Avenue El better than anything short of a re-ride on it from Coenties Slip to 125th Street.

Lawrence and Lothar Stelter have done what few authors and photographers could possibly have accomplished; they have brought the Third Avenue El back to life.

For myself and the thousands of other train buffs in captivity, I can only offer one more word, THANKS!

Stan Fischler

ACKNOWLEDGEMENTS

Larry Furlong, Marjorie Goldberg, Tiger Lilly Lee, Barbara Millstein [Brooklyn Museum], G.E. Van Wissink, Florence Eichin, Alice Lundorf, Ralph & Lois Myller, Robert Presbrey, Ross Klein, Leonard DeHart, Stan Fischler, Joe Franklin, Brother Thomas Trager, S.M., Jack LaRussa, Janet Behrmann, John Henderson, Peggy Buckwalter, Barbara Cohen and Judith Stonehill [New York Bound Books], Deborah Shinn [Cooper Hewitt Museum], Alice Frelinghuysen [Metropolitan Museum of Art], Nate Gerstein, Joe Cunningham , Clara Lamers and Miriam Karais [Brooklyn-L.I. Historical Society], Jane Shadel Spillman [Corning Museum of Glass], Isobel Aronin

DEDICATION

In memory of **Irene Asch Foltz**,
who first interested Lothar Stelter in photography and the El.

PREFACE

At the midpoint of the 20th Century, New York City stood poised as the "Capital of the World." The new Atomic Age had dawned. The headquarters of a new international organization for the post-World War Two era, the United Nations, had been established in the city. More importantly, the post-war consumer boom and its abounding prosperity had its key decisions made in the corporate and advertising headquarters in the canyons of Manhattan Island. Yet, on that very island, a thoroughfare harkened back to another age; it retained its distinctive aura despite the momentous changes in the city and the world. This book is about Third Avenue and its elevated structure during the early 1950's. The structure, known as the "El," the stations and trains en route radiated a special feeling and charm upon the neighborhoods adjacent to it. A young man appreciated this atmosphere and he endeavored to capture the scenes on film. The collection in this book represents the definitive work on the El in its later years and the first to be completely in color.

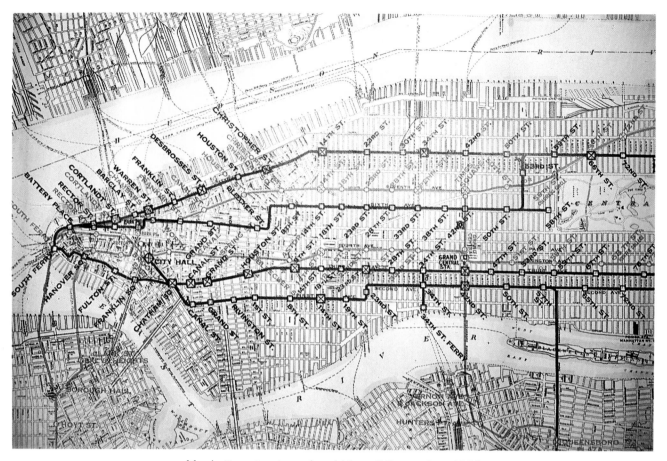

Manhattan streets and rapid transit lines, circa 1924
Note: Only IRT routes are shown with the Elevated lines in blue and the Subway lines in red.

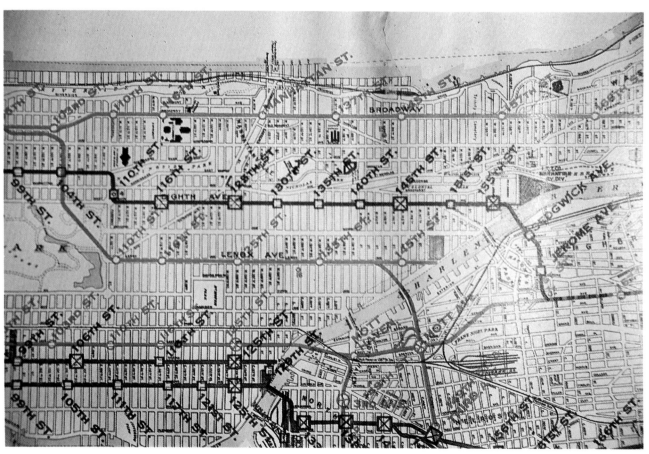

BRIEF HISTORY OF MANHATTAN ELS

Since the beginning of European colonization, the region in the vicinity of New York Bay has been very prosperous. Trade, the trans-shipment of goods and ideas, enabled the region to grow and attain an ever-increasing standard of living. Industrialization fueled growth and expansion in New York at sometimes exponential levels. As the population spread, people worked, worshiped and recreated in places distant from where they lived. Thus public transportation developed. The horse-drawn coach, or omnibus ("for all") appeared in 1832. The horse car, a horse-drawn vehicle that ran on rails, appeared soon thereafter. After the Civil War (1861-1865), the horse car network became inadequate to serve a population which was approaching one million. Civic leaders sought a means of transportation that would be separate from and unimpeded by the congested streets.

Beginning with an experimental cable-drawn line in 1867, an elevated railway system developed. By 1876, one route ran along Greenwich Street and 9th Avenue from Battery Park to 59th Street. The steam-powered trains made the run in thirty minutes and 2,012,953 passengers rode the line in the year ending on October 1, 1876. **Rapid Transit** had arrived in New York, and the expansion of the elevated system complemented the city's expansive growth. The New York Elevated Railroad built a line on 3rd Avenue and upgraded the 9th Avenue line. The Gilbert, later Metropolitan, Elevated Company, built a line on 6th Avenue and by 1880, a line on 2nd Avenue. In 1879 the companies merged to form the Manhattan Railway. During 1879, the steam-driven elevated system reached 155th Street in northern Manhattan. The system became especially popular when the flat five cent fare was instituted on all routes at all times on October 1, 1886. [The fare remained five cents until 1948.] The four main lines, plus shuttle routes on 34th and 42nd Streets carried 3,134,806 passengers in the first week of November 1886. Also in 1886, the 3rd Avenue line was extended north of the Harlem River into the Annexed District, later known as "The Bronx."

The burgeoning metropolis grew and teemed more than ever as the 20th Century began. New and better technologies by 1900 had heralded initiation of construction of an electrically powered underground rapid transit service, the Subway. The Manhattan Railway also electrified its lines and in 1903, the elevated system was leased for 999 years to the Interborough Rapid Transit (IRT) Company, the operator of the new Subway, which opened in 1904. Concurrently, population growth continued unabated and immigration peaked. During the early years of the 1900's, New York truly became a world class city. The elevated system accommodated this growth with longer trains, new express services on the 2nd, 3rd and 9th Avenue lines and expansion into Queens over the 59th Street Bridge in 1917. The subway system expanded even more in Manhattan and the other boroughs. By 1920, ridership on the Manhattan Elevated system reached the highest level it would attain. During the teens, the population of Manhattan ebbed and 1920 would be the last census in which Manhattan was listed as the most populus borough.

No sooner at its greatest extent, the elevated system began to contract. Short spurs were closed in the 1920's. Changing economics and perceived public needs choreographed a long term public policy to remove elevated lines as soon as possible and preferably replace them with subways. The drop in ridership due to the 1930's economic depression and concomitant political changes spelt the doom of the Manhattan Elevated system. In December 1938, the 6th Avenue line closed and was completely demolished by April 1939. The replacement subway opened in December 1940. After protracted negotiations, the City obtained the IRT Co. in June 1940 and closed the 9th Avenue line south of 155th Street and the 2nd Avenue line north of 59th Street. Both lines were demolished in 1941. [The City-operated 8th Avenue subway had opened in 1932.] The remainder of the 2nd Avenue line was scrapped in 1942. By the end of World War II, only the 3rd Avenue line survived in Manhattan.

CHAPTER ONE: THE THIRD AVENUE EL AS AN EDIFICE

Any story of Third Avenue must of necessity begin with a detailed look at the El that ran above it. That imposing structure, which was as much a signature of New York in the first half of this century as its skyscrapers, shaped the character of the people alongside it and the thoroughfare that ran below it.

Josephine, the photographer's wife and painter of the picture at the left, shares her husband's fascination with New York memorabilia. Evidenced by her presence here at the 76th Street station, in 1953, while accompanying him on another photo expedition during their courting days.

STATIONS AND STAINED GLASS

Local stations on the El had a station house on uptown and downtown sides. The wooden platforms were long enough for a seven car train and were partially covered with a highly decorated cast iron canopy. One or two stairways descended to the street. For some unknown reason, all stairways at 67th Street descended onto Third Avenue instead of the side street. The northbound stations at 34th Street and 42nd Street stations had an odd stairway that descended to the avenue rather than the side street. Only 59th Street station had an escalator, and it had unusually shallow treads. Newsstands often occupied the space beneath the stairway. The honor system prevailed at these well- stocked newsstands. Merely toss your coins on the counter and the newsstand man would oblige. The stationhouses had hardly changed in 70-odd years. Windows abounded with ornamented stained glass. Red. Blue. Orange. Floral patterns and geometrics. Intricate and delicate patterns were sculpted in the cast iron railings and friezes on wood trim. Coal-fed pot-bellied stoves kept the waiting rooms toasty warm on cold days. Most of the turnstiles were GE electric models from the 1920's. "Errr-dink-dink-dink-KLUMMMP!" they proclaimed upon accepting a nickel (through 1948) or a dime or beginning in 1953, a token for the 15 cent fare. The uptown 47th Street station had a single turnstile which the change clerk released when one paid the fare.

It is known that the Cornell Iron Works produced much of the decorative ironwork. Noted artist Jasper Francis Cropsey designed the ironwork and stained glass for the 6th Avenue El and it served as a prototype for the architecture of the other elevated lines. John Hertz, a draftsman from Switzerland, was on the staff of the Chief Engineer Courtright of the New York Elevated Railroad. He apparently designed the stations of the 3rd and 9th Avenue lines after the gable-roofed chalet buildings of his homeland. [The station houses on the 2nd and 6th Avenue El lines had a hip roof amidst similar ornamentation.] The structure and the stations withstood the tests of more than seventy years of use and in later years, neglect. (cont. next page)

(left) Despite the sign, coin-operated electric turnstiles were adopted in 1922.

(right) This intricate iron-work is representative of a bygone era. It adorns this station stairway, and the worn wooden door testifies to its age.

(below) At 84th Street station, the multi-colored glass and woodwork are 1878, the turnstiles are 1922 and the lady's attire is strictly 1950's.

Ornate, decorative ironwork was a hallmark pf the Victorian Era [1837-1901]. Some recent efforts to duplicate the work of the late 19th Century craftsmen have encountered difficulty. Some historians have suggested that the problem stems from the fact that contemporary ironworkers learn their trade as adults. By comparison, the 19th Century artisans were apprenticed to the trade as youths, a time when the bones of the hands and wrists are still flexible. Thus, the techniques required to form intricate patterns were learned and perfected early. While it is, of course, possible for adults to learn the same techniques, the task requires more time and effort to master.

(above) The coal stove and ticket booth at the 47th Street station displays an earlier form of turnstile; and it was the only one of its kind still in use, in the 1950's, on the 3rd Avenue El .

(right) The glowing coals in the stove at 18th Street station keep the waiting room toasty warm on a frigid winter day.

(left) The Victorian proclivity for skillfully executed ornamentation extended to this ceiling piece. It originally held a lighting fixture.

The intricacy of the glazier's art for the masses is evident in this transom.

FIGURES MOMENTARILY FROZEN IN STAINED GLASS

A young lady checks her modern hairdo in a
reflection framed by the Victorian glazier's art.

On a snowy day, a man in a "Manhattan cap" has just lit a cigarette as he leaves the El station. The ornamented glass could not be replaced by this time; hence, the clear glass on the left. The stone New York Central railroad viaduct looms in the distance.

(above) Morning sun highlights Victorian woodcraft and ironwork of the station and adjacent buildings at 53rd Street. [In 1995, none of these buildings will remain.]

(below left and right) Ornamental ironwork was a hallmark of post-Civil War (after 1865) construction; the El was no exception as this platform railing illustrates.

(above) The interplay of light and shadow at 34th St. station is fixed in time by the advertisement for "On the Waterfront" which was released in 1954.

(left) The worn wooden platform resounds to the footsteps of this El patron; the long afternoon shadows symbolize more than the end of the day. The sun is setting on a mode of transportation: the El.

(right) The wood and iron canopy of 28th Street station harkens back to a bygone era in railroad station design.

(left) Modernism by the El from 34th St. station: The Chanin Building (1929) and the Chrysler Building (1930) typify the Art Deco architectural style while the Chrysler Building Annex (1952 and by the El) at the right typifies the International Style.

(right) The contrast between the 1950's art of the Savarin coffee ad and the worn wooden doors bespeak the passage of seven decades.

Behind these three waiting passengers is yet another contrast. The colorful Victorian glasswork versus the glowering face of the advertisement.

From the 34th Street overpass, we glimpse a variety of lives. Note the brown-uniformed station attendant keeping the platform tidy, the man with the hat box glancing uptown, the turquoise scale doubling as a luggage rack, a rider sitting on the sand box, two ladies chatting and others scurrying about. The platform layout was different at the north end of 34th Street station because the 34th Street shuttle connected with the main line at the top of this view before its demolition in 1931.

THE STRUCTURE

The original 1878 structure of the El was an open webbed iron girder riveted to an iron pillar and bent arch. The ties and catwalk were of wood. The tracks power, (or "3rd") rail and railing, were of steel. The tracks ran on an average of about twenty feet above the avenue. The center express track, which was installed in 1915, was supported by a steel plate girder. Some found the darkness created by the structure depressing and uninviting. However, on many a hot, sunny day, the trellis-like pattern provided a welcome shaded environment. Artists and photographers have likewise portrayed the patterns of the shadows in their respective media.

(right) In this bustling street scene under the El, the *New York World-Telegram & Sun* International truck makes a delivery to a local newsstand at 67th Street and under the El stairway. The *NYW-T&S* will outlive the El for only a decade. Note the 1941 Buick.

Dr. Michael Kudish, a professor at Paul Smith's College, was born near 3rd Avenue on the Lower East Side and lived near the line during most of his boyhood. As a boy, he often rode the line to visit his father's office which was located in the vicinity of the 47th Street station. During a December 1994 interview, both he and his mother, Esther Kudish, shared some reminiscences about the El. A typical trip began at Tremont Avenue in the Bronx where they boarded a downtown local. Upon entering the first car, he headed immediately for the front window alongside the motorman's operating position, an action which was instinctive for New York City boys as soon as they were tall enough to reach the glass.

As for that portion of the line which was closed by the mid-1950's, there were several locations that left lasting impressions.. "Just below the 149th Street station, the line left 3rd Avenue on a sweeping curve and ran above private property. The local tracks were below the express level, and they were jammed against the side of the buildings, which created the feeling that the train was traveling through a sort of tunnel. There were station stops at 143rd, 138th, and 133rd with platforms on both levels, but I never saw anyone enter or exit, and I always wondered why there was express service at these points. I later realized that they were remnants from the days when there was more industry in the area. After leaving 133rd Street, the tracks entered a doubledeck swing bridge to cross to Manhattan.

"Leaving the bridge, the tracks turned west into the 129th Street station. The severed stub of the 2nd Avenue El could still be seen, a fact brought to my attention by my father who used that line. If you were to exit the train at 129th Street, you would encounter an ancient open gate car sitting on a track stub on the opposite side of the platform. A fascinating relic to me, my father told me that it was used for training motormen and conductors.

"After leaving 129th Street, the line became a three track route over 3rd Avenue. Just before 89th Street station, we would pass the Ruppert Brewery on the easterly side of the El. It was a huge building with great glass windows which showed the huge kettles inside. Being a young boy with no interest in beer, I thought that huge vats of chocolate milk would be of greater interest. On occasions, we got off at 84th Street and walked to the Metropolitan Museum of Art. Most of the time we stayed on to either 53rd Street or 47th Street to meet my father at The Chartist Studio where he worked as a commercial artist.

"After having dinner at some eating place such as the Automat, we would head home, and often on the express which had a fast straight run from 42nd St. all the way to 106th Street. I always thought it was strange that there was no stop at all at 86th St. which is such a major street. We did take the uptown local at times, and I well remember one time the motorman failed to make an accurate stop and several cars overshot the station platform at 53rd Street. We had to wait while the conductor made sure that no doors could open over empty space! The exiting passengers in the front had to move back to the rear cars to leave, while we entered at the rear and then moved forward. The motorman may have had a momentary distraction which caused the problem, because we weren't delayed while any repairs or inspections were made.

"Although I was most familiar with the line above 42nd St., I recall several points along the line which were of interest. At 34th Street, there was a pedestrian crossover which could be seen from 42nd Street. The express stop at 9th Street served Wanamaker's huge department store. We used to travel to South Ferry to take an excursion to Staten Island, but most of the trains ran to City Hall terminal so we had to get off and wait for the second if not the third train before getting one bound for South Ferry. the route to South Ferry was short but interesting, a great winding "S" curve at Coenties Slip and passage beneath one of the stone arches of the Brooklyn Bridge foundation.

"I remember that the line was arrow straight from 129th Street all the way to the Lower East Side, and that was unusual for any city transit line. There were three basic services: Locals from City Hall or South Ferry which ran to Tremont Avenue [177th Street] or Gun Hill

Road; and the Local-Expresses, which were express in Manhattan and local in the Bronx to Gun Hill Road; and, the Through-Expresses which ran express in both Manhattan and the Bronx. I rode most of the services but never the downtown express, at least not that I recall. I do remember the changes as the cutbacks took effect: the closure of South Ferry, then the City Hall spur, and finally the elimination of night and weekend service below 149th Street. I did ride it with my family when the line closed in 1955.

"When I was old enough to travel with my friends, we developed a game based on the car numbers. I don't recall the details now, but we assigned points based on certain duplicating or consecutive numbers say 1717 or 1234. To earn points, we had to stand at a good viewing spot, watch the train come in and then race to that car as it came in. We made various rules which had to be followed in order to score. Just one of those games which boys make up to amuse themselves and compete with their buddies."

Dr. Kudish is a professor in the Division of Forestry at Paul Smith's College in Paul Smith, NY and is the author of several works including "Where Did the Tracks Go: Following Railroad Grades in the Adirondacks."

A heavy, wet snow blankets the structure, yet it fails to slow this uptown local as it approaches 89th Street station.

THE 'EL' AND THE SNOW

The snow changed the scenery along the El. As the photographer recalls: "The El sounded different, muffled, in the snow."

(left) Earlier in the same snowfall, three boys play in the curb slush in front of the same store featured in the previous photo.

(next page) Amidst the falling snow, this Yorkville lady goes about her daily chores by the El. The illuminated street light is centrally controlled; its being on indicates an expectation of more stormy weather ahead.

(right) Three ladies make their way southward at 89th Street. That Merc and Olds at the curb would not be out in weather like this today had they survived.

(left and below) A train departs 84th Street station, while in the photo below the 84th Street El station wears a mantle of white.

(above and below) Neither snow nor rain nor gloom of night prevents the intrepid photographer, Lothar Stelter, from enduring the misery of standing on the express train platform, at 125th Street, early in the morning to record this mood scene. The signal forecasts clear track ahead for the next southbound express.

Meanwhile, this is the street scene from the upper level/express platform. Two blocks west, a New York Central train pauses at the 125th Street rail-road Station. A 1950 Buick and a 1950 DeSoto taxi-cab fend their way through the slush and snow.

As snow muffles the sounds of the city and the STS Mack bus lumbers uptown at 90th Street, the El provides fast and dependable transportation.

EN ROUTE THE 'EL'

By the time Lothar Stelter had started to record the El on film, the two track branch to South Ferry via Pearl Street had been closed and demolished. The most southerly station was the enclosed, copper-clad, City Hall station which had two levels, four tracks and six platforms above Park Row and next to the Municipal Building. 2nd Avenue trains had used the upper level until 1942 and 3rd Avenue trains used the lower level until the station closed on December 31, 1953. The next stop was Chatham Square. Once the junction of the 2nd and 3rd Avenue lines, until 1942 the station complex had eight active tracks, four platforms and two levels. From Chatham Square to 129th Street, a seven mile length, the 3rd Avenue line had three tracks. The three express stations on the Bowery had two island platforms. Local stations had platforms on the east and west sides of 3rd Avenue. Express stations at 9th Street, 23rd Street, 42nd Street, 106th Street and 125th Street had a pair of platforms built at a higher level; the structure "humped" at these express stops Express trains ran southbound in the morning and northbound in the afternoon rush.

The El had a laudable safety record. Few accidents occured throughout its many decades of service in all types of weather. The Great Blizzard of 1888 caused only one death. This was remakable given that the local tracks lacked a signal system and inherent safety features! The express tracks had block signals. Fires were also rare among the wood cars, platforms and station-houses heated with coal fires. For example, on June 16, 1953, a downtown local struck the kerosene lamp of the preceeding train at 34th Street and caused a small fire.

PASSENGERS & ROLLING STOCK

(previous page) The weather-beaten exterior of car #1152 denotes decades of service in all types of weather.

(this page, top) A Bronx-bound local train stops at 84th Street. The weather is warm; the roof clerestory vents are open, but the gentleman are attired with hats and suits.

(this page, bottom) The uptown local has arrived! In this clear view at 34th Street station, one can almost smell the creosote on the ties and hear the throbbing of the air pumps. It is easy to imagine the clicking of the shoe heels on the wooden platform, the clack of the doors closing and the whine of the traction motors accelerating as the train pulls away from the station.

(left) Going home on the El...This view is probably near the end of service in the Spring of 1955 for the closure notice is taped on the window.

(below) A typical five car set of MUDC's with an uptown local at 59th Street station. The open rear door provides plenty of light and breeze to make for a comfortable trip home. Photo by Robert Presbrey

ROLLING STOCK

Most of the electrically-powered cars and trailers that remained in service by the early 1950's dated from 1903 to 1911. The manufacturers were Saint Louis Car, Wason, American Car & Foundry, Jewett and Cincinnati Car. The steel-framed, wood-bodied cars had gates at their end platforms removed and the ends enclosed and powered doors (The "MUDC" on the blue signs in the stations stood for "Multiple Unit Door Control") added in a 1923-24 upgrading. A few sets of former 1903 BMT cars that had been rebuilt for the 1939-40 World's Fair plied 3rd Avenue express runs. The seats were weaved rattan or "straw." Leather straps were provided for standees (hence: "straphanger"). Fresh air entered the cars from clerestory vents in the roof. All told, it was a comfortable way to travel.

(below) A summer scene at the rear door. A rubber fitting on the top chain prevents damage to the glass when the door is closed.

(upper left) A lady waits patiently for an uptown local at 34th Street station and two riders enjoy the cool breezes in the rear vestibule of an uptown express.

(upper right) An uptown express train pulls away from 133rd Street [Bruckner Blvd] station in the Bronx. A well-dressed gentleman surveys the route travelled from the open rear door. A red STS GMC bus heads south on Willis Avenue. Note the link-and-pin coupler that was standard on Manhattan Elevated cars and similar to the couplers on the old Hudson Tube [now PATH] trains.

THE REAR DOOR

In those days, before air-conditioned transportation, summer months heralded the opening of the door of the last car in the train. The open door, sometimes halfway ajar, afforded the lucky rider a cool, refreshing ride; and the drama of the city unfolded before oneself. The three chains barred exit; a rubber piece appended to the top chain prevented breakage.

CHAPTER TWO: A TRIP UP THIRD AVENUE

NEIGHBORHOODS & LANDMARKS

Along most of 3rd Avenue were residential areas: Brownstones (townhouses), tenements, elevator apartments, "walk-ups" and a few post-1945 housing projects. Almost all of these were attached. In midtown, office buildings loomed and some stood along the tracks. While Bloomingdale's department store was at 59th Street, most businesses on 3rd Avenue were "Mom-and-pop" operations or franchises of larger chains.

Third Avenue was famous for its pawn shops, antique stores, bars and restaurants, including the Automat at 42nd Street. In 1954, there were a dozen pawn shops and over 100 antique shops and galleries on 3rd Avenue. More then 100 Irish bars lined the avenue between 21st and 90th Streets alone. Numerous restaurants, luncheonettes, eat-in bakeries and ice cream parlors made 3rd a place to eat for people of whatever social standing if not an epicurean's delight. Fire escapes clad the facades, and television antennas were sprouting from the rooftops. The sun dried thousands of families' wash. Parking meters had been recently installed, yet ample parking was available. Other businesses included drugstores, hardware stores, radio (&TV) repair shops and specialty shops for keys and sportsmen. Chatham Square terminal was in the heart of Chinatown. The biggest industrial establishment was the Ruppert Brewery at 92nd Street. Passing train riders could observe the huge brewing vats and kettles. Import shops, movie theatres, cigar and candy stores, and street clocks were found along the avenue. Liederkranz cheese was invented, by Emil Frey, at the Tode cheese shop at 1028 3rd Avenue near 61st Street and first tried out on the New York Liederkranz men's choral society at 58th Street to rave reviews, hence its name. Cooper Union, the art and engineering school, abutted the El at the south end of Third Avenue. Further south on the Bowery was New York's Skid Row.

The *New York Daily News*, with a circulation of 2.5 million, called 42nd Street near 3rd Avenue home. It had more than twice the circulation of any newspaper in the nation. In the United Nations, also at 42nd Street, many saw a better world order. Nearby were the supermarkets, ice cream parlors, Chinese laundries, pushcarts and stands. All very useful features for a very civil population.

All, by the El.

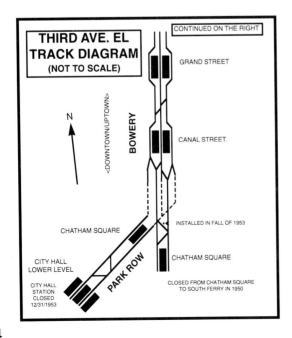

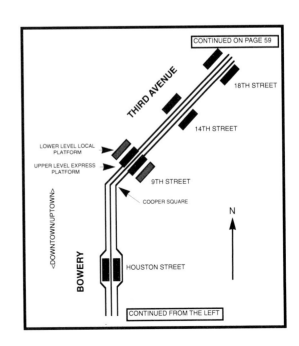

(right) While not technically on 3rd Ave. proper, the City Hall terminal of the El marks what most people consider to be its beginning since the El is the chain that ties the neighborhood "pearls" that were strung along side it together. This imposing copper-clad structure is the City Hall terminal. Only the lower level is still in service. The Municipal Building towers on the left. Let's slip past those vintage parked cars in the foreground, scamper up the stairs and take a ride uptown.

 CHINATOWN

(below) As the sun sets on a tepid summer evening it still bakes the abandoned [since 1942], refuse strewn Second Avenue El platform. Having left City Hall terminal, a 3rd Avenue train which utilizes the platform in the rear approaches the Chatham Square complex in Chinatown. Of course, being on the edge of Chinatown the Venice theater featured American films and the Silver Star theater featured Chinese films. On the street rolls a plethora of [what would be considered antique vehicles by today's standards] cars with a 1953 Studebaker going past the Star theater, while a 1936 Ford and Ford truck are passing the Venice theater. Across the street are parked a 1950 Cadillac with a 1953 Olds in front.

(left) We are looking north from the Chatham Square station that served as the El's southern terminus after 1950. This photo was taken during the brief period between the closing of the South Ferry Branch and the closing of the City Hall branch. The tracks and junction with the 2nd Ave. El can be seen on the lower level to the left of the photo. In the distance an uptown express from City Hall is entering the Canal Street Station. During this brief period the station was single tracked with a spring switch for a turnback. When the City Hall branch closed, the second track was restored, and two crossovers were installed.

When this complex was reconstructed in 1916 from a simple crossing, the project made world-wide engineering news. The IRT Company noted with pride that 1,836 daily trains were operated on schedule throughout the reconstruction project.

(below) In this view from our train on the City Hall branch, we see a local train which has terminated at another platform of the Chatham Square complex. In the foreground and beneath the train lie the abandoned platforms once used by 2nd Avenue trains. The level beneath the train served 2nd Avenue El trains prior to closure during 1942. The housing project beyond is the Alfred E. Smith Houses, completed in 1950 and named for the former Governor of New York State.

(above) Looking south from Canal St. station towards the Chatham Square complex, we see a fan trip over the line pocketing in what was once the express ramp to the City Hall Branch. The rust on the downward ramp tracks indicates they are out of service since the branch was closed. This trip took place shortly before the end of service in 1955. The interlocking tower that controlled this once complex junction is on the lower level in the distance to the left of the train, which is made up of "Q" type cars. These "Q" cars were originally rebuilt for the 1939 World's Fair service. ROBERT PRESBREY

THE BOWERY
LOWER EAST SIDE

(left) This view north from Canal Street shows the long row of flop houses and sleazy bars that made the Bowery infamous. Notice the crossovers between here and the Grand Street station. Houston St. station is visible in the far distance, with an express at its center track. A southbound local is approaching Grand Street.

Enis Sarro lived at 55 Mulberry Street in "Little Italy."

"I lived near The Bowery and shopped there as well as on the lower end of 3rd Avenue. I remember the many hotels for the unfortunates that stretched to Grand Street. [Her son, Tom, remembers the sidewalks of The Bowery; packed curb to building with thousands of 'bums' (the term used to describe the down and out before the politically correct 1980's), most suffering from acute alcoholism. At Division Street there were coat stores such as Brenner Bros. and at Catherine St. a small A&P. There was, and still is, a Bank of America and Bowery Savings Bank along with the Diamond Exchange at Canal Street. Near Grand Street was Fischer Studio where my wedding pictures were taken.

After Grand Street there were many dry goods stores and wedding shops; particularly Marlene, where my daughter Loretta, daughter-in-law Angela and I bought our wedding dresses. Houston Street area contained, and still does, many lamp and appliance stores.

On Park Row there was the Venice theater and after O'Rourke's Bar at Chatham Sq. there were many wholesale toy stores. Across the street from O'Rourke's was Schullers Mens Shop and upstairs the Minniwanna Club. Maizie was the cashier at the Venice theater and she was well known in the neighborhood. Maizie also owned the Carousel in Coney Island. There was a Childs Restaurant and across the street St. Andrews Church, and on the next block was Maxie's Busy Bee, a very popular place that offered waffles with ice cream for 5¢."

(left) In this view north from Grand Street station, 20th Century skyscrapers stand in the distance and in stark juxtaposition to the aging relics of the 19th Century on the Bowery.

Actress Helen Hayes reminisced about the El running through The Bowery in her autobiography, *On Reflection*:

"...Then there was the remarkable elevated train that passed people's windows like a magic carpet—so near that you could say hello to the fat mothers who leaned on the window sills with babies, or the thin old men in bathrobes who sat staring at the world passing them by...."

HOUSTON ST.

As Isabel Cunningham would say (pgs. 64-65). Looking from the "stuffy darkness and boredom" of the eastern entrance of the 53rd. and Lexington IND subway station towards the "stimulating" 53rd St., 3rd Avenue El station.

ROBERT PRESBREY

(above) Looking north from the Houston Street station towards Cooper Square and Cooper Union College as a downtown local approaches. Cooper Union, an art and engineering college, was founded by Peter Cooper in 1859. Fourth Avenue which forks to the left past the college was a center for used book shops and sometimes referred to locally as "Book Town."

COOPER SQUARE
LOWER EAST SIDE

A downtown El train turns off 3rd Avenue and onto the Bowery at Cooper Square near 6th Street. Cooper Union, an art and engineering college founded by, Peter Cooper (whose statue sits in the typically triangular New York "square") in 1859, stands west of the El, while a STS Mack bus is about to head northward under the El. It is 5:50PM This being the later years of the El, the train service will cease as the evening commences. Note the STS bus dispatcher's booth and the motorcycle parking in the "Safety Zone."

Carmen Dempster, a retired architect, recalls:

"Reminiscing about the time of the 3rd Avenue El and my trips to school at Cooper Union is quite nostalgic. I lived in upper Manhattan or [Central] Harlem, specifically 116th Street and 8th Avenue, which meant I had to take a trip downtown and then crosstown to school.The other option was taking a crosstown bus on 116th Street to the El and then downtown to Cooper Square."

"Riding the El was an experience in itself, as it gave me an opportunity to be above ground and see everything from a higher level. Spring, summer and fall were marvelous as you were out in the open air, no air-conditioning, so windows were open and the sounds and smells of the city were very apparent. It might be old

and dirty, but I didn't notice."

"The trip took me by many tenements, and it was interesting for me to see different people in their windows. It was fun to be able to glimpse inside the homes and wonder what was happening and what their lives were like inside."

"Once downtown, the El was a part of our life at Cooper [Union college]. It was a place where you had lunch from the vendors: ice cream, hot dogs etc., who sold their wares beneath the shadow, of the El. Inside the school, the "El" was still a presence. It wasn't too bad in the studios, art, sculpture and drawing etc., where after a while you became used to it; but, the lecture hall which was on the 3rd Avenue side of the building took the major assault."

"I remember many times, Dr. Zucker would be in the middle of a lecture and would have to stop because he couldn't be heard. there were times you wondered if we were going to be shaken apart. But, 'Cooper' is still there and the El is gone."

Looking southward, Cooper Sq. viewed from Cooper Union College shows an uptown local taking the bend onto 3rd Ave.. That's the Houston St. station in the distance, and the center track ramp to the express platforms at 9th Street is on the far left.

Ron Tagliagambe grew up on Saint Mark's Place between 1st and 2nd Avenues. "[The El] was always there, yet I never rode on it. My mother warned me to stay away from the derelicts who came up from the Bowery and hid behind the El pillars. You could see the El from my house, and as a kid I took a picture of it. I remember the shadows on the street. And then, it was torn down. I still live in Manhattan in the teens and go back to the old block once in a while..."

And from John Simak, who lived on Saint Mark's Place (8th Street) between 2nd and 3rd Avenues: "The most unique thing about the El was the stations. The attendant, or today we'd say token seller, would light the coal in the pot-bellied stoves. They must have had a sheet metal cover over the wood floors. I always wondered why they didn't catch fire. I remember 9th Street station near Cooper Union. Riding it was fun like all elevateds; go to the front car and be above the street.

"The El made noise and lots of it. On our block was the Polish National Home. Between the noises we could hear the El and the Polka bands at the Home, we did not get much sleep on weekends.

"I do not recall the glass in the stations or the demolition. My family moved to Nassau County in 1959. It was a good neighborhood then. I now live in Rosedale, Queens, yet I go back to the Odessa Restaurant in the old neighborhood now and then."

A couple of employees have just climbed the stairway from the local to the upper express level at 9th Street as a southbound local departs. Notice how the express platforms are built over the local tracks with a platform on each side because this track is bi-directional. The center track was added years after the original construction. Third Avenue was not as wide as The Bowery, so there was no room to widen the trestle.

9th St. station is a typical express stop with two levels. The famed Wanamaker's department store rises in the background. The early episodes of the Captain Video TV series are broadcast from the DuMont TV network studio in Wanamaker's store. On the left the 1949 Chrysler convertible is being passed by a 1947 Ford and the green Checker cab on the right is passing a Chevy panel truck and a 1951 Plymouth. A red and cream STS Mack bus heads southbound under the El.

(left) An uptown local train has just passed this typical pawnshop and drugstore at 12th St.

(right) Three passerbys peer into the trove of items for sale in that same pawnshop. $5 for an overcoat!

Lets take a walk up Third Avenue. Need eye glasses? Should we buy fishing tackle? Fishing tackle at 3rd and 14th! People are probably used to catching a few fish on Third but not of the finny variety. Should we browse like the young couple, perhaps newlyweds, looking to pick up a few things that they need on a short budget at the Gramercy Exchange next door or perhaps get something repaired by Mr. Messite or a new set of keys? If all that shopping tires you out, we can always stop to get something to eat at the corner or have our shoes shined by one of two young entrepreneurs, providing we can hear ourselves think as the elevated trains brake to a stop at the station overhead. This seeming endless variety of establishments packed close together was typical of Third, and this meant inhabitants of the area did not have far to go to get everything they needed.

GRAMERCY PARK
BELLEVUE

(right) A push cart peddler, typical of those found up and down 3rd Avenue. This one at 14th Street sells snacks— peanuts, fruit, bread etc....

(below) The same corner viewed from 14th Street shows more businesses in the same line of trade illustrating the intense competition that business faced. Note the variety and spice of urban life, how the utilitarian, ethnic and cultural converge: an olive drab US Mail truck, a Pechter's (bread) truck next to a 1949 Pontiac, watch repair, Hungarian dining room, a pair of 1951 DeSotos at the near curb with a 1952 Buick Roadmaster in motion and the famous Academy of Music [movie theater] across Third Avenue. The famous German restaurant, Lüchow's, is next to the Academy. Shall we choose to go into the underground station of the 14th Street Canarsie Line and head crosstown or out to Brooklyn and Queens, or shall we go upstairs and head either uptown or downtown?

(previous page) Standing at the north end of the southbound platform at 14th street. We peer telescopically at the 18th Street station and the 23rd Street express stop. On the avenue we see more of the plethora of German-lineaged restaurants, whose pantrys and meat lockers are supplied by trucks like the 1954 Chevy you see in the foreground. Note the 1955 Chevrolet Bel Air crossing 3rd at 17th Street in the distance.

(above) This is the uptown stationhouse at 18th Street, typical of the local stations of the El that have hardly changed in seven decades. Parked on the right, the north side of 18th Street nearest 3rd, is a 1948 Pontiac fast-back, a 1936 Ford V8 less its front grill and a 1947 Plymouth with an outside sun visor unlike the visor-less 1947 Plymouth on the south side. Further west approaching 3rd Avenue and the corner florist shop is a 1949 Mercury and a 1947 Pontiac. Looming on the left is the mansard-roofed headquarters tower of the Guardian Life Insurance Company at 17th and 4th Avenue [it will become "Park Avenue South" in 1959].

(right) Waiting patiently for the uptown train at 18th Street. The station shows the wear of three-quarters of a century of use.

23RD ST.

MURRAY HILL
KIPS BAY

(previous page, top) South from the 23rd Street express platform, we see an approaching express train has overtaken a local at 18th Street. The red arrow points to a radio repair shop. Such shops are common in an era when radios represent a substantial investment for a family.

(previous page, bottom) The uptown express has departed 23rd Street. The young man at the open rear door, intent on his newspaper, is oblivious to the passing cityscape. The pedestrians below are equally intent upon their tasks. Note the continuation of the parade of ethnic restaurants, food stores and the repair shops so typical of Third Avenue. This area is a center of the city's Armenian community.

(this page, top) 23rd Street has long been one of the city's major thoroughfares. Only the 3rd Avenue El offers express as well as local services. The Metropolitan Life tower duplicates the Campanile in Venice while the El station was modeled on a Swiss chalet. A right-hand drive foreign [how unusual!] car double parks at the left; it is a French-built Talbot. Domestic makes line the street: a 1950 Pontiac "woodie," a 1947 Mercury coup, a 1949 Dodge, a 1937 Plymouth, a 1946 Plymouth, a 1950 Pontiac, a 1950's Buick, a 1947 Buick Caravan, a 1950 Dodge Diplomat and under the El is a 1950 Nash and a 1949 Oldsmobile.

(right) Shoeshine boys wait and scour the area for potential customers under the El. Informal dress, sneakers and a changing work ethic have made scenes like this obsolete.

(above) A northbound local rumbles past 24th Street, which was then a quiet residential neighborhood. The absence of automobiles attests that most residents used public transportation. The new 1955 Oldsmobile *88* and the 1954 Plymouth taxi is a harbinger of the changes to come. The presence of horse manure, from horse drawn street peddler wagons or policemen on horseback, trolley tracks, and cobble stones harken back to a simpler age.

ROBERT PRESBREY

(previous page, bottom & this page) Two views of an uptown local departing 28th St. station on a warm and sunny afternoon. The Chrysler Building and Annex and the *Daily News* building tower in the distance. The old tenements reverberate with the passage of the local train. Note the juxtaposition of eras delineated by the cast-iron trim of the station platform canopy. Note the old semaphore signals protecting movements on the express track. The local tracks were not signalled.

(previous page) You might have your pocket watch repaired at 28th St. or have a Coke at the fountain in the candy store. Note the 1951 Ford and 1950 DeSoto taxicab. The Bellevue Hospital complex at 1st Avenue can be seen in the distance.

(above, left and right) Steins and things in a store window at 29th Street and 3rd Avenue.

(below) A teeming neighborhood scene at 31st Street by the El. On the northeast corner we see the candy store which has a soda fountain; around the corner is an "Express" Chinese laundry. To the right of the photographer is a parking lot. [Later the site of the Kips Bay branch library.]

Beauvais Fox, a retired professor, recalled a time when he rode the El to his place of employment in the Financial District. He boarded at the 34th St. station, which was located near his home on East 37th Street near 5th Avenue. Although he sometimes rode the subway, the El provided better access to his office near Wall St. "I used the Hanover Square station which was a small narrow 'island' platform between the towering office buildings of the Wall Street area, the effect being that of a train curving through a mountain pass."

"Each part of the line had unique characteristics, many of them linked to the past. For example, at the 42nd St. station, there was a crossover passageway below the station which was divided so that it could be used by both those who had paid their fares and those who had not. A convenience for both El passengers and street pedestrians, it was a remnant of a connection to a shuttle service which extended west along 42nd Street to Grand Central. The shuttle had closed in 1924, but the passage remained until the El was demolished. There was a crossover above the tracks at 34th Street which served the same purpose; access to a shuttle service that extended east above 34th Street to the Long Island Railroad ferries. That service ended in 1930, but the crossover remained until the end. Unlike the one at 42nd St., the bridge at 34th Street was accessible only to paid passengers. In point of fact, passenger crossovers were rare, a fact which led to one of the more foolhardy actions of my youth.

"It was the wee hours of a winter night during the Depression; and I realized that not only had I missed my station but also any chance to cross to the downtown side. I faced a long boring ride uptown to a major station where I could have crossed over, plus a wait in the cold for the next southbound train and than the ride back. It was the Depression, and one didn't waste nickels, so the option of simply getting off at the next station and paying another fare to get back was out of the question. I did get off at the next station but waited until the line and platforms were clear. I then used the crew steps to descend to track level and cross all three tracks to the opposite side. The tracks were

dark, and each was fitted with a live third rail which, unlike those in the subways, were exposed at the top and sides. Some had a protective barrier on the side but it offered minimal protection. The things we did to save money in the Depression! Well, I survived, but I don't recommend that procedure as an economy measure!

[Beauvais Fox is retired from the Dept. of Mechanical Engineering and Aerospace Technology at the Polytechnic Institute of Brooklyn]

Turning the view slightly to the north we see the neighborhood at 31st Street has an A&P supermarket and the *Daily News* building at 42nd Street which has its own television tower for *Daily News*-owned TV station WPIX, Channel 11.

MIDTOWN
TURTLE BAY

Looking west at 34th Street at the reconstructed station house. Shuttle trains once ran to the Long Island Rail Road ferries at the East River. After the shuttle's demolition in 1931 this was the unornamented, utilitarian result. The angular cut in the stationhouse is there because of the curving connecting track. The shuttle platform abutted the flat wall of the stationhouse. The yellow and green GMC busses of the 5th Avenue Coach Co. [a private franchised operator with routes in Manhattan and Queens] manuver eastward as does the Chevy approaching us.

(above) The intersection of 34th St. and 3rd Ave. is a beehive of activity. A *N.Y. World-Telegram & Sun* truck makes a delivery to one of the newsstands under the El while a 1950 Oldsmobile trails behind. The green Buick Roadmaster is a rare 1949 Riviera hardtop, the first of its kind. The air-conditioned movie theater offers "It Shouldn't Happen To You" and a cool respite from the heat and activity. This scene is from 1953.

34TH STREET OVERPASS

From 1879 to 1930, an elevated line ran along 34th Street from 3rd Avenue to the East River where connections were made with Long Island Rail Road ferries. Even though the shuttle route had been demolished, an overpass at the 3rd Avenue station remained in place. It offered the photographer a convenient vantage point to observe and record operations.

(previous page, bottom) Meanwhile back on the El, we're looking south, a rush hour crowd is gathering at 34th Street station as an uptown express speeds past. The passengers in front are enjoying the breeze and the view on this hot day. The motorman was supposed to discourage this practice at the front end of the train. To the left of the front car of the train is a signal cabin that controls the set of crossovers south of 34th Street station.

(this page, top) As Robert Presbrey looked north from the overpass he simultaneously photographed an arriving and departing local. The 34th Street ferry shuttle connecting track once came in just north of the uptown platform on the right.

(left) The funeral of British King George VI, Queen Victoria's great-grandson, fills the back page of the *Daily News* in 1952. The attention of this 3rd Ave. El rider is focused elsewhere in the newspaper.

Nighttime at 34th Street station.

Virginia Pensabene grew up on 3rd Avenue until she moved with her family to Queens in 1925. In the early 1950's she, in effect, returned to the old neighborhood when she worked at Norcross Cards on 34th Street between 1st and 2nd Avenues. Although she did not use the El then and merely passed it en route to the 6th Avenue Subway, she specifically recalls that in May 1955 "the girls [in the office] from the Bronx missed their ride on the El each day. They hated having to take the subway. The subway was horrible, just terrible compared to the El."

Bella Shutz was born and raised on the East Side of Manhattan. For more than thirty years she was the superintendent of various buildings, mostly dwellings on the East Side, until retiring across the river to Queens in 1977. "Manhattan was such a pleasure then. There were so many stores and movie theaters. My favorite bakery was Fred Bunz's at Houston Street and the Bowery, by the El, with the pineapple pie. Lüchow's [German restaurant] was at 14th Street; my husband once received an invitation to a Christmas at Lüchow's. 3rd Avenue had its jewelers and pawn shops. You'd pawn your watch or radio if you needed money and we'd say: '2-to-1-you don't take it out!' [someone would buy the object].

"I know the movies: the Academy and the RKO Jefferson at 14th Street, the Regent at 28th and the Superior at 31st. Some of the movie theaters on 3rd Avenue were so small, you could watch the movie from the sidewalk! My oldest son was in a stroller and kept pestering me to stay put so he could watch the picture. I also remember going in and around the pillars on 3rd Ave. with the baby carriage. When the El came down in 1955, I was at 36th Street between

2nd and 3rd Avenues. I took my youngest son down to the avenue to see the El coming down. It was not a bad area even then; you could walk at night.

"I used the other Els too, the 2nd 6th and 9th Avenue Elevateds when they were running. The 9th went to Paddy's Market. I even remember trains that had gates and not doors. When I was a young girl on the Lower East Side, every time the El train passed by, it turned the light on in our apartment four floors up! My mother demanded to know who put the light on and sure enough, the El train went by and on it went! Those were the days!"

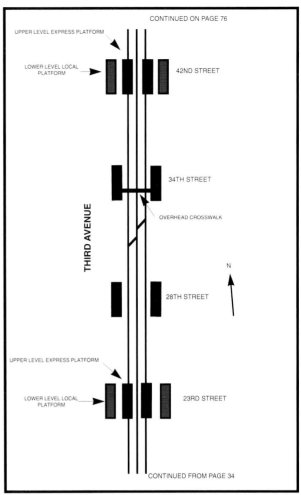

CONTINUED ON PAGE 76

UPPER LEVEL EXPRESS PLATFORM

LOWER LEVEL LOCAL PLATFORM

42ND STREET

THIRD AVENUE

34TH STREET

OVERHEAD CROSSWALK

N

28TH STREET

UPPER LEVEL EXPRESS PLATFORM

LOWER LEVEL LOCAL PLATFORM

23RD STREET

CONTINUED FROM PAGE 34

Thaw! The sun is out, the snow is melting and a transit worker with safety flag in hand crosses the tracks at 34th Street

The key of the locksmith shares the sky with the Chrysler Building and Annex, and the El near 40th Street.

Barbara Millstein, Curator of Photography, Architecture and History at the Brooklyn Museum, remembers the ornate Manhattan El stations as a girl. Later she used the 3rd Avenue El "all the time" to get to one of her early jobs as a copygirl at the *Daily News* at 42nd Street. "Even during the 1947 snowstorm [the blizzard that set the record for snowfall in the city], the trains never stopped. I just plowed my way through [on the El] and got to work."

Westbound traffic on 42nd Street is backing up. Meanwhile, the 1952 Chrysler Building Annex rises across 3rd Avenue and the El. Businesses on the north side of 42nd include a florist and an E.J. Korvette outlet with Zenith radio and TV signs in the window. The Farberware truck may be making a delivery from the firm's plant in the Bronx. The photographer is standing with Central Commercial High School to his back. Down toward 3rd Avenue, we see a barber shop offering 60 cent haircuts, a Marco Polo's (a chain of Italian restaurants) with a tempting menu on a red sign attached to the sidewalk canopy and a competing eatery, one of the famous Automats. Parked in procession on this side of 42nd Street are a 1949 Buick, a 1950 Chevrolet convertible, a 1947 Chevrolet, a 1953 Chevrolet and a lemon colored 1953 Studebaker Hawk. In the westbound traffic are a , #1564, a 1948 GMC STS bus, a 1951 DeSoto taxi, a 1949 Plymouth Suburban [the first all-steel station wagon], an early 1950's green and white Checker cab, another DeSoto taxi and a 1952 Cadillac. Two other red and cream GMC STS busses have progressed further across 42nd Street. The year is 1953.

(previous page) The newly completed United Nations building rises in the distance; it is the hope of the new age. The 1878 ironwork at 42nd Street station survived to see the Cold War. The ubiquitous Automat, a staple of New York diets, will survive to almost the end of the Cold War. [It will close in 1990, the last Automat in operation in New York.]

(this page, top) South on Third Avenue from the stairway to 42nd Street station in 1954. Four years earlier, shortly after New Year's 1950, these streets were filled to the brim with excited children and their loving and patient parents. The occasion, a visit to the News Building across the street by Hopalong Cassidy. The line started on the west side of 3rd Avenue at 42nd Street, turned the corner and went down the west side of 3rd to 30th Street, across the street and back north on the east side of 3rd to 42nd Street and into the Daily News Building. A crowd of this magnitude was not anticipated, and it took many hours to wend one's way along that line. Hopalong Cassidy paraded in an open car up and down 3rd Avenue to the delight of the youngsters who were waiting to shake his hand at the News Building.

A downtown local train has just left the station. A cigar store occupies the southwest corner at 41st Street. At #651 3rd Avenue is Mr. Olsen, a violin maker. The excavation on the right is for the new headquarters tower of the Socony [**S**tandard **O**il **C**ompany **o**f **N**ew **Y**ork]-Vacuum Company which will change its name to "Socony-Mobil Oil Company" before completion. Service on the El will have ended by then.

(right) The 42nd Street station stairway provides an ideal noontime perch for the many "sidewalk superintendents" that were on duty that day.

Looking west on 42nd Street from the 3rd Avenue El station, we see the excavation for 150 East 42nd Street, the new Socony-Mobil Building in 1954. We also have a broadside view of the Lexington Avenue facade of the Chanin Building (1929). To the far right are the lower floors of the 77 story Chrysler Building (1930). The limestone and brick building to the left of the Chrysler Building is the Hotel Commodore. Crossing 42nd Street at Park Avenue is the vehicular bridge of the Grand Central Terminal complex. From 1878 to 1923, the El had a shuttle service that ran from here to the railroad depot. The building on the far left is the entrance to the IRT Queensboro or Flushing Subway. There is a paper ticket transfer from that line to the El.

Isabel Cunningham is not a native New Yorker, having moved to the city at age 27. Though she had visited relatives in the area previously, her perspective on the El was different. She did not commute on public transit on a regular basis, but walked from her home in Tudor City in the East 40's to her employment as art director at I. Miller Shoes on 40th St. and 5th Avenue. Her only use of the El for work was on days when the streets were filled with the slushy remnants of snow. On those occasions, she used the pedestrian crossover at 42nd St. to avoid the mess and heavy traffic of the intersection. She did ride the El but for a purpose which was more pastoral than the daily commute which was the sole purpose of most passengers.

For her the El was a unique and fascinating way to see the city. "It was always there when I passed on my way to and from work., but I never really had time to think about it. On a Sunday, I had time and decided to ride it to the end of the line just to see what was out there. I was not disappointed. The stations were vintage and seemed warm and friendly in comparison to the cold tile of subway stations. In winter, the potbelly stoves added an additional note of antiquity. The old wooden cars with their narrow windows, heavy wooden seats and leather straps were almost rustic in character. The ride gave you a sense of being away from the dense city at the very moment that you were passing some of the most congested areas. At the same time, it gave you a panoramic view of the city. On a warm day with the breeze blowing through the open train windows, it seemed almost surreal. I traveled to the end of the line in the Bronx, and I recall getting off and strolling through what must have been Bronx Park.

"On another occasion, I traveled down to South Ferry, and that was a ride you would remember. It seems we were well above the rooftops as we passed Chatham Square, then the train was dwarfed by the buildings near Wall Street. The most impressive part was the great curve near Pearl Street. The train curled around the curve with a sort of mechanical grace and then arrived at South Ferry. Suddenly, you felt that you were away from the city as you looked out at the water. The station was a little narrow structure which seemed cute and very appropriate to the quaint character of the whole El. On other occasions, I rode down to Chinatown for dinner with friends who were native New Yorkers, or at least had lived here longer than I. They were eager to point out some of the more interesting features of the line: the old stations with potbellied coal stoves and stained glass windows, the many branches and spurs which had been closed. Some of the cars could be entered only through a gate at the end of the car, like an old railroad car.

"For those who had to use the line every day, I'm sure that it wasn't so interesting. For me, it was an opportunity to enjoy a part of the character of New York, that character which made New York the subject of songs and stories. By comparison, there were subway stations all over Midtown, but I never felt any desire to ride one just to see where it went. Subways were for getting to a specific destination quickly. The El was different—when you stepped down you were stimulated; on the subway you had to climb up from the stuffy darkness and boredom. The El provided an open air ride above the city and yet still was part of the fabric of urban life at its most intense."

A southbound local accelerates away from the 47th Street station as a lady [in those days it was not proper for a lady to be seen in public without a hat] ambles down 45th Street towards 3rd, possibly heading for the A&P across the street. Note the maroon 1948 Nash *600* on the street at the right. The early 1950's Jaguar Mark 1 [foreign makes were very uncommon in this era] shares space in the lot with a 1951 Dodge.

A DeSoto taxi heads northward and over the trolley tracks [the last streetcars ran in 1946] at 45th Street. A REA (Railway Express Agency) truck is parked southward. The shop at the northwest corner of 46th Street sells General Electric fans, de rigueur for summer cooling, (along with fire escapes). In this era air-conditioning is reserved for commercial establishments like theaters or upscale homes. Besides, most of the apartments on 3rd at this time are not wired to handle these units. The Ballantine P.O.N. [for Port of Newark (NJ)] truck is probably making a delivery of beer to the A&P supermarket between 45th and 46th Streets on the east side.

Rosemary Wagner has lived all of her 58 years in the Upper East Side of Manhattan. Although not related to Mayor Wagner, she sometimes received his mail! While she describes herself as slightly claustrophobic and usually rode the bus, "..the El was nice, real nice. Everybody took it. It was open; the sunlight coming through. [It was] cold waiting in the winter. The stations were so old with wood banisters and the old fashioned glass with a reddish tint. The trains were nice and old, too. They should have left it that way. I used to meet my husband-to-be under the El. He took the El to Gleason's Gym in Harlem to box. The El got you where you were going fast! Safety was not an issue; you'd ride at any hour.

"Shopping on 14th Street, Klein's and May's, were a big thing. Other shopping was 86th Street with W.T. Grant's, the mom & pop stores, pushcarts and of course, Papaya [King]. There was lots of bars of different ethnic groups, yet no fights like today. The stores were little. For 25 cents you'd go to the movies: RKO, Monroe, Annex, Loew's...We also had block parties. On Sundays we were on the El to go to Coney Island or sometimes Rockaway. They were hard, but beautiful days; I'd go back tomorrow to those days. We didn't think we lived in a slum. It was better then; we had more family.

And it was all by the El.

[Gleason's Gym was actually in the Hub area of the South Bronx]

Don't you feel you can mingle with the crowd on the corner on this warm afternoon by the El? The City has installed a new street light at 46th Street amidst the busy avenue. The "Quiet" is for a school on the side street. On the east side of 3rd Avenue is a Chinese laundry and Joe & Rose's Restaurant while a delicatessen is on the west side. Your voice is raised as you speak to your companion over the rumble and screeching brakes as the uptown local enters the 47th Street station. Further noise is being generated by the STS Mack bus handling downtown surface transportation. The Chevrolet parked at the corner hails from New Jersey. Note its unusually sized license plate.

A lady ascends to the uptown 47th Street station which serves the Midtown business district on a warm and sunny day. A newsstand does a brisk business under the El stairway and near the bar on the right. A 1954 Mercury moves westward in the distance.

This well-stocked newsstand beneath the stairway to the downtown 47th Street station is typical for 3rd Avenue. Perhaps the chic young lady lives in the upscale Buchanan apartment house across the street? The print media reign supreme still. *Look, Women's Home Companion, and Collier's* are among the publications for sale. Baseball great Willy Mays of the **New York** Giants is featured in *Time* magazine

(previous page) Looking south from 49th Street towards the 47th Street El station we see a much seedier street than one would encounter there today. Notice the wheeled carts for the garbage cans. Oh, that garbage on our city's streets today is handled so kindly! That's real wood on the Oldsmobile station wagon and another Oldsmobile, a convertible nearer the curb.

(above) Notice how the different kinds of business establishments seem to repeat themselves block after block. The three gold balls is a world-wide symbol of a pawn shop. Lewis Jacobs at 59th Street is one of many on Third Avenue. The fish lures the sportsman; the eateries lure the hungry, and the marquee lures the movie-goer. The Original Joe's Restaurant was the second Joe's on the same block. "Original" helped differentiate them. The photographer's bicycle is parked on the sidewalk near the 1953 Chevrolet convertible. Note the old style wire waste basket.

Adele Gordon has made Yorkville her home since 1917: "Born on 82nd Street and lived on 83rd Street for the last 43 years.

I rode the 3rd Avenue El alot. We went to Chinatown and the Bronx Zoo; it was safe to ride then. I remember the colored glass in the stations at 67th and 76th Streets. 3rd Avenue had pushcarts as well as stores. Miles at 86-87th Streets and Loew's Orpheum at 85-86th Streets. We went to Bloomingdale's and yes, I remember the escalator to the 59th Street station. I have pictures of taking the El down. My friend who lived on the Avenue was glad the noisy El was gone, yet others were sad. This was always a good neighborhood. Taking away the El has not made much difference." [The Orpheum was actually between 86th and 87th Streets.]

Parking meters have appeared as evidenced in this view looking north from 59th Street. Off-street parking can be had for 75 cents. Laurence Olivier was starring in the main feature a 1948 revival of *Hamlet* at the Baronet Theater. Note the 1950 and 1953 Buicks with their trademark holes on the front fenders.

(above) The view uptown from a southbound local departing 59th Street station. The tall building on the left is Bloomingdale's department store. The white building at 66th Street is Manhattan House, a luxury apartment house built in 1952.

(below) The downtown side of the 59th Street station with its unique Bloomingdale's sign on the station roof and the all-weather enclosed escalator with the unique wooden treadles in the left foreground. Nothing too good for a "Bloomies" customer.

(previous page, top) The view out the rear door of an uptown express as it roars past Bloomingdale's at 59th Street station. The Chrysler Building pierces the sky at 42nd Street. Awaiting uptown passengers are engrossed in their newspapers. The approaching uptown local train is at 47th Street station, while a downtown local is at 53rd Street station. Note the escalator at the right on the downtown side. The Baronet movie theater featured Sidney Granger in "Wild North," a 1952 release.

(previous page, bottom) Having spent the afternoon at Bloomingdale's, homebound shoppers mingle with early rush hour travelers. The red-orange candy and gum machines will disappear from the NYC transit system in the 1970's.

(left) More passengers waiting on the same platform

(below) On the platform opposite Bloomingdale's department store at 59th St. waiting passengers survey the scene. Elevated passengers have more to amuse themselves with than subway riders.

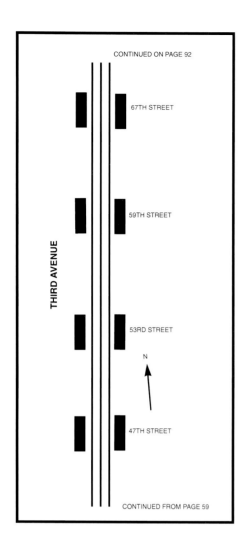

CONTINUED ON PAGE 92

THIRD AVENUE

67TH STREET

59TH STREET

53RD STREET

N

47TH STREET

CONTINUED FROM PAGE 59

LENOX HILL

66th Street is also a "Quiet" area as the hospital sign announces. Similar signs are placed near schools. The DeSoto taxi travels upon Belgian paving blocks, and the owner of the corner building has sold the window spaces for advertising.

67TH ST.

(previous page, bottom) North from 66th Street about 1953 and the trolley tracks are emerging from the asphalt paving. On the west side, we have a hardware store, Carney's bar and a seafood restaurant with a black 1951 Chevrolet, a black 1952 Cadillac, a 1950 Buick and a Willys at the curb. The red Diamond-T Eastern truck is turning onto 66th Street. Before we reach the uptown 67th Street station, we will encounter a delicatessan and an ice cream parlor with its "Coke" sign on the right. Parked at the eastside curb from near to far a 1947 Pontiac, a 1949 Olds and a 1949 Plymouth among others.

(this page, top) Looking south the 67th Street station, the Midtown skyscrapers appear smaller the farther north we go. The northbound local approaches the station as it enters the Lenox Hill residential neighborhood.

(right) Another newspaper stand nestled under the 67th Street station stairway.

(above) The boy at the rear door of this uptown local enjoys the summer breezes and a lofty view of the bustling street scene at 72nd. Street. The 1954 GMC truck is probably making deliveries in the neighborhood. We also see a 1954 Mercury and a 1951 Ford convertible evince that people enjoyed open air travel like the El rider above. A Willys Jeep heads southward in back of the truck in this late 1953 view.

(below) Looking north from 73rd Street. This shows the narrowness of the traffic lanes. Many accidents with passengers boarding and disembarking from the busses helped fuel the fires of those intent on removing the El..

South from 76th St., 3rd Avenue's businesses carry the usual potpourri of items: Irish imports, Chinese laundry, Cuban cigars and the requisite paper litter on the street....

(above) The 76th Street station is nestled in amongst the high-rise buildings that have grown up around it. The imposing church in the upper right of the photo is the Roman Catholic Church, Saint Jean Baptiste. In the 1950's it was possible, from the obervation deck of the Empire State Building, to keep a 3rd Ave. elevated train in view about 60% of the time as it wended its way up or downtown. If it existed today, the El would be almost invisible from that vantage point.

(below) Looking northward from 75th Street at the back end of a southbound local. At 79th Street in the distance, the El will pass between a pair of substantial 1920's era luxury apartment houses.

A southbound local approaches 76th Street station while multi-generational shoppers stroll past the myriad businesses on the avenue. Detroit's Big Three have several products on 3rd: in front on the right is a 1954 Buick, a 1947 Plymouth, a 1954 Mercury, a 1953 Ford station wagon and a Dodge truck further back.

Joe Cunningham, a transportation and engineering historian, recalls his memories of some of the Yorkville stores which were located in the vicinity of the El and which thrived for decades on the pedestrian traffic which was engendered by the El. "My favorite place was located on the east side of the Avenue a few blocks south of 84th St. station. I first discovered it on a frigid night about a week before Christmas. A brilliantly lighted display window featured an elaborate assortment of Lionel electric trains, and within the store, long showcases displaying a full range of train sets, accessories and everything else that a boy might wish. These was also a working layout, and the owners were always friendly and allowed you to linger as long as you wanted. I'm not sure when it closed, but I do know it lasted until the early 1960's. Closer to 84th St. station, was the fascinating shop of a man who made violins, a fitting companion to the numerous German restaurants which featured live music.

"Another boyhood obsession was electronic and mechanical gadgets. Just north of 86th Street on the westerly side of the Avenue was an electronics store which featured German audio components with names which were as interesting as the devices: Telefunken, Nordmende and Loewe-Opta, plus a host of others which I have long forgotten. Just across the street was a large Woolworth's which was always fun to peruse and was the source of some last-minute Christmas Eve "stocking-stuffers" that are now treasured memories. Adjoining the 5 & 10 was a huge W.T. Grant's which was a young boy's delight. The basement sales level featured a selection of hardware, lights, pet supplies and even some HO trains which kept me coming back every time my mother did any shopping in the area.

"If you wanted something to eat, there was a plethora of choices. In addition to the fine German restaurants and dining halls which included live accordion music, there was that "old-reliable" of the city, the Automat and a terrific White Tower hamburger store at 86th Street. The area was also home to numerous variety, thrift and similar stores which held little interest for a boy. There was, however an unwritten agreement: if I exercised a little patience, I could spend equal time at the trains, hardware or electronics which could not have entranced my mother to the extent that they did me.

"Although the El did not stop at 86th, its presence was felt in more ways than just heavy steel girder work. The vitality of 3rd Ave. and the numerous commercial establishments were a legacy of the El which began with the opening of the line in 1878. Though still a major commercial strip, the redevelopment that followed the demolition of the El has changed the character of the area. Now filled with upscale shops, the area is one of the most exclusive in the city. While good for the urban economy, there is no gain without some loss; in this case, that of the old "neighborhood" small businesses. I, for one, am glad to have been able to experience a small bit of "old" New York which even then, was fading rapidly.

YORKVILLE

(next page, top) Third Avenue is replete with store signs. No doubt some of them originated at this 84th Street shop. Near 84th Street station is the former Yorkville Turn Halle, the German athletic club. Across 3rd Avenue on the southwest corner, there is a "Going-out-of-business" sale underway; and on the north side of 84th Street, we see a garage which also sells Tydol-Flying "A" gasoline.

(next page, bottom) A southbound local arrives at 84th Street while a northbound local is at 89th Street station in the distance.

ROBERT PRESBREY

(previous page) South from 85th Street, a young lady passes the landmark street-clock and pawnshop, and later a bar and restaurant.

(right) Lunchtime view of the 85th Street clock as a northbound local train zips by. [In 1995, it will remain minus the three gold balls.] The clock was in a scene in the 1945 film *The Lost Weekend* with Ray Milland.

(below) Another fixture: the pushcart vendor. It's two <u>pounds</u> for a quarter at 85th Street. (not two <u>each</u> for 25 cents!) The orange sign of Papaya King [a tropical fruit drink] at 86th Street can be seen through the pillars at the left as well as a photo shop and a corset shop. On this side of 3rd, we see a Kraft cheese truck making a delivery, an old style wire waste basket, a green mail box for deposit of general mail (not storage) and a branch of Manufacturers Bank. At the corner is parked a 1951 Dodge. Across 85th Street is a 1954 Chevrolet and a 1952 Willys.

(previous page) A bird's eye view of the happenings at the corner of 87th Street. All the classic elements that constitue a 3rd Avenue cityscape are here. Note the uncovered third rails typical of the El as a local rumbles and grinds its way southward. Former New York City Mayor, Robert Wagner, was born in the corner building out of the picture, to the left of the green Buick.

(above) At 89th Street, northward: Hans's bar, mattresses and bedding, a barber, "air-conditioned" spaghetti & pizza(?) which is more important?.... Near the hydrant is a 1948 Chevy and ahead of it a 1951 Ford.

(left) Although the structure is low at 89th Street, the sloping Manhattan terrain necessitates three long flights of stairs to reach the station house on the El and also a deep foundation for the tidy building with its tan "gravity-type" fire escape on the right. A man checks the trunk of his late 1940's Buick as a Cadillac and Pontiac drive by. As you head west of 3rd, the scene quickly changes to many storied luxury apartment houses. The station agent has all the windows in his tiny office open to catch whatever breeze may be blowing on this hot mid-summer day. It is 1953, and Eisenhower is President, Dewey is Governor, and Impellitteri is Mayor.

(above) During a quiet moment at 89th Street station, the street scene below attracts the attention of this passenger. He passes up the bread advertisement.

(above) The late afternoon shadow of the 89th Street station canopy highlights the boy who is savoring the ride on the uptown express.

(right) North from 89th Street in Yorkville. The Ruppert Brewery stands at 91st-92nd Streets. Note the Rexall drug store, the Paradise Club bar and the store that sold trunks, presumably for long sea voyages or railroad journeys.

Looking north from an 88th Street rooftop. A Bronx-bound local approaches 89th Street station and will soon pass the Ruppert Brewery. In the distance to the right, the white structure is the new Metropolitan Hospital at 97th Street and First Ave. which opened in 1952. Parked on 3rd Ave. are a 1950 and 1948 Pontiacs, a 1941 Chrysler, another 1950 Pontiac and further down, a 1946 Plymouth. A Rexall drug store at 89th Street with its blue and orange sign serves the area. Notice Wankel Hardware is next to Hans's Bar.

Karl Wankel is the proprietor of Wankel's Hardware store at 1573 3rd Avenue between 88th and 89th Streets. The Wankel family has owned the business since 1896 and it is one of the few establishments that have survived since the time of the El. "I was born in the neighborhood; it was mostly German and Irish then. The dust from the El would cover the shelves in the store. The El was at the lowest point, eleven feet, in the city outside of our store. Once a truck full of chickens struck the El and the whole neighbor-hood had chickens [for dinner]. Both of my grandfathers once ran to catch the El at 89th Street to go up to the Bronx to visit my father-in-law. One of them had to make change, missed the train which carried my other grandfather uptown and was stranded on the platform because my other grandfather knew where to go!"

"I remember the pushcarts on 86th Street and as a kid waiting in a dentist's office and watching the passengers getting on and off the El trains at 89th Street station. The cobble stones streets like on 3rd Avenue were very slippery."

The block where Wankels Hardware is situated is one of the few rows of tenements that are intact on the east side of 3rd Avenue and Mr Wankel, who is also president of the local hardware association, sighs; "Progress. In the high rise towers today are mostly upper class-yuppie types. Retail and wholesale business is always changing. There are few of us from the old days like Yorkville Vans and Scanio Moving. Krauss Hardware at 84th Street is still there, but Mr. Krauss died years ago and his widow sold the business. The bars changed, yet some kept their old ways. I remember Schaffer's at 89th Street still had nickel beer and a free lunch counter in 1945!"

Yorkville residents go about their routines at 88th Street and at #1571 Wankel's harware store in its sixth decade of business in the neighborhood. On the same block, we have a mattress/drapery shop, a pork store, Hans's bar, a stationery+candy store and Peter Pan dry cleaners. *Nutri-Cola* utilizes the top of one of the buildings for advertising to El riders. At the northwest corner is a parking meter and an empty parking space. The 11'-0" clearance causes the structure and passing train to dominate the scene. The white 1950 Chrysler has no problem passing under the El nor will the 1953 Pontiac or the occasional horse drawn wagon. However, the photographer has seen trucks stuck under the structure on numerous occasions.

(**above**) view of and into the Ruppert Brewery at 92nd St. from a northbound express train. Note the huge copper kettles for brewing the Ruppert beers and ales, such as *Knickerbocker*. The brewery dining hall attracted many who lived and worked by the El.

(**below**) Commemorative charm for the passing of the El from the Ruppert Brewery

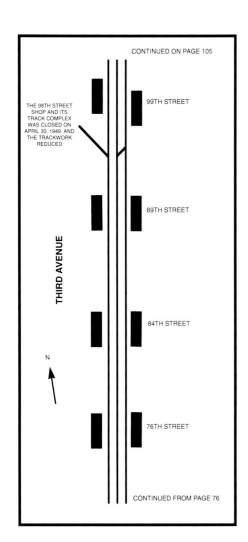

CONTINUED ON PAGE 105

THE 98TH STREET
SHOP AND ITS
TRACK COMPLEX
WAS CLOSED ON
APRIL 30, 1949 AND
THE TRACKWORK
REDUCED

99TH STREET

THIRD AVENUE

89TH STREET

N

84TH STREET

76TH STREET

CONTINUED FROM PAGE 76

(next page) Although hazardous in event of fire, opening fire hydrants is a time honored way to beat the New York summer heat. These boys at 95th Street are keeping cool!

(below) North from 99th Street station about 1953. The state-of-the-art structural engineering of 1878 dictated the use of this style of cross bracing where the tracks ran high above the thoroughfare. Soon the red and cream northbound STS [Surface Transportation System, a private franchised bus company with routes in Manhattan, the Bronx and Westchester] 1948 Mack bus will assume all public transit services on 3rd Avenue. A police officer on foot patrol stands in a building entrance on the left while a lady with a baby carriage heads northward in this 1953 scene. The dump truck next to the maroon Ford on the right at 100th Street is heading for the construction site of the new housing project east of 3rd Avenue. The photographer has often frequented the German eat-in bakery to the left. Note those spiffy whitewalls on the pre-war Buick parked southward on the left.

Karl Stricker was raised on Melrose Avenue and 153rd Street near the Hub in the South Bronx. He and his family rode the El on shopping trips to 14th Street (May's and Klein's), 34the Street (Macy's and B. Altman's) and 42nd Street (Stern's). Sometimes the family went to a German restaurant in Yorkville's 86th Street via the El. Uptown destinations on the El included the Bronx Zoo, Fordham Road shopping and the Botanical Gardens (200th Street station).

"I used to meet my dad at the 149th Street station when he returned from work in Midtown. In order to avoid the traffic at the Hub, I crossed over on the El station. My father was not happy at taking the subway after the El closed south of 149th Street. On many a hot, muggy summer nights, it was nice and reassuring to hear the trains go by and to know it was there. It was fun to go to the front and 'drive' the train. I liked the whine of the motors and the imprints the rattan seats made on my knees after kneeling at the window and watching the passing scene. I remember smelling the hops from the Ruppert Brewery as the train passed by."

"Everybody liked the El; nobody said they were glad that it was gone. The El did not deter shopping. It brought people to the Hub area. It was vital, the spine of the Bronx. The neighborhoods were homes of working-class people and not slums. Rather than improving the corridor along 3rd Avenue in the central Bronx, getting rid of the El did more to kill the area. With some maintenance, it would still be there. [Demolition] may have helped in Manhattan yet those buildings could have been built with the El.

"I rode on the last train in Manhattan in 1955 and the last train in the Bronx section in 1973."

The 99th Street El station northbound platform. Notice the north and southbound platforms are staggered to allow for the 98th Street Yard leads to enter the line south of the southbound platform. The shop building is still used by the Transit Authority as a repair shop for turnstiles and the retaining wall still supports the Lexington Houses.

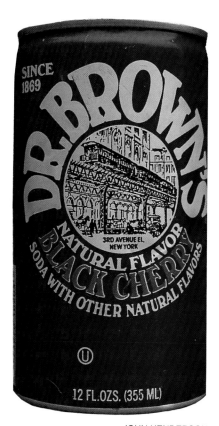

JOHN HENDERSON

Despite the near-universality of electrically-powered refrigerators, an ice man still delivers to customers in the vicinity of 100th Street and 3rd Avenue. As the ice man makes a delivery, his horse waits patiently with the wagon. Note the parked Kaiser to the right of the horse and the DeSoto taxi passing on the avenue.

(next page) Viewed from a building at the southwest corner of 100th Street and 3rd Avenue, an uptown local train traverses the high cross-braced structure as a ubiquitous red STS [Emblazoned above the windows is the company slogan: "Ride the Surface Way"] Mack bus passes in the other direction with a Pontiac and Willy's panel truck following. It is 1953, and the incumbent Mayor is seeking another term as evidenced by the billboard on the side street [Impellitteri was not re-elected.] Shortly after this photo was taken the building on the far right was torn down to make way for the George Washington Houses, housing project.

Behind the ice block in the lower right photo lies a special serrated shovel, one of the tools of the ice man's trade.

Maria (born Gandia) Safina spent her childhood years in East Harlem:

"We lived on the first floor of the J.E. Johnson Housing project at 2070 3rd Avenue at 114th Street. Our windows looked up at the El and its shadows. I remember the wicker seats on the trains. We rode the El to go to S. Klein's at 14th street, where everyone else shopped for clothes. 3rd Avenue had lots of stores and other attractions. At the corner grocery, Scafuri Brothers Self-Service Market, at 114th Street, we would buy Borden's (Elsie the Cow's) Milk in bottles.

After my father died in 1953, my mother had to go to work. With our nearest relatives in Puerto Rico and lacking fulltime daycare, my mother would send my brother and I to the Cosmo movie theater on 116th Street just off 3rd Avenue each and every weekday for the entire summer! She would pack us lunch, and we 'reported' to the matrons at the theater. There, we watched the same feature films and newsreels over and over again! But we were safe and secure, and the matrons knew us well."

"East of 3rd Avenue was mostly Italian, while our area was mostly Hispanic and Black. [In the early 1950's] You could walk on 3rd Avenue and the side streets after dark. Crime and drugs would only became a serious problem later. Later we moved to Long Island City, Queens and when I got married, it was off to Brooklyn!"

(above) Looking south down 3rd Avenue from 101st Street the no longer used trolley tracks have not yet been covered over completely, only rail joints have been patched over. Complete repaving will wait for the demolition of the El.

(below) Looking across the temporary lots waiting for the George Washington Houses to be built, we see a southbound local slowing for the 99th Street station. Notice the Studebaker Hawk, Packard and Nash "bathtub style" Rambler among the cars on the other side of the street, along with the red and cream GMC STS bus on 3rd Avenue.

Sidewalk food vendors are another time honored tradition in New York City neighborhoods. This "hot dog man" shares the corner at 104th St. with an ancient lamppost that was a veteran of the gaslight era. The lamplighter of that time rested his ladder on the cross-piece while lighting the lamp.

(Previous page, top) After a long run from 42nd Street, express trains stop at 106th Street in East Harlem, a residential area. Auto traffic is still so light that this wide street lacks a center dividing line. We see a pair of Pontiacs with their distinguishing chrome stripes in the foreground. The barber shop pole is to the right and a few doors down the California Cafeteria. Across 3rd is a Thom McAn shoe store, and across 106th at #1915 3rd Avenue is the red and gold sign of a S.H. Kress 5, 10 & 25 Cent store near the newsstand beneath the El stairway and the parked Ford and black Chevrolet. The greenery of Central Park lies in the distance. A kerchieffed lady jaywalks north across 106th while an interesting character with a cigarette walks eastward on a sunny day in 1953.

(Previous page, bottom) "Wash Lines" a typical scene of city domestic life viewed everyday from the El.

(below) Viewed from the roof of a building, a southbound local arrives at the 106th Street express stop. A small piece of the 116th Street station can be viewed in the distance courtesy of this telephoto shot.

Gary Grahl, a retired schoolteacher, recalls: "I was born and raised near the El in the Bronx; I was always near it. It was very important in the lives of people and it especially served as a connecting link among the German-American communities of Yorkville in Manhattan, and Morrisania, Tremont and Bedford Park in the Bronx. Families, friends and ethnic organizations such as singing societies and athletic clubs were connected by the El.

"We lived near 177th Street and took the El to visit my grandmother at 99th Street in Yorkville. As a kid I watched the train movements in the 98th Street yard. When my mother went to her workplace at 42nd Street and 6th Avenue (Stern's department store), she chose to ride the 3rd Avenue Through-Express; it was faster than the 6th Avenue Subway on the Grand Concourse.

"We were all sad to see it go [service to Manhattan]. I took a day off from college on May 12, 1955 and rode on the second to the last train. As I exited at 177th Street station, I picked up a CHATHAM SQUARE destination sign, my souvenir of the day. I also rode on the last train in 1973, a fan trip on April 29. The Bx55 bus service in no way replaced the El."

116TH ST.

(below) South from 116th Street station; a departing downtown local is passing 115th Street [exactly where demoltion will begin in August 1955] and the J.W. Johnson housing project. The pedestrians cast long shadows from the mid-morning sun. On 3rd Avenue, shoppers have a "Food Shop" and a Jewelry store that sells Bulova watches and has an optometrist on the premises. "El Enchanto de Las Mechachas" (The Beauty of the Girls, a beauty parlor) serves the new Spanish-speaking clientel.

(above) Passengers gather on the northbound platform at 116th Street station.

(below) North of 116th Street, trackwork is underway. The approaching downtown train has its front door half-opened for better ventilation on this hot day. Many furniture stores line the avenue in East Harlem. Watertowers emblazoned with company names, such as the green one, are fixtures of the New York skyline.

Manuel Rey, a retired data systems specialist, grew up on 74th St. near Lexington Avenue. He and other boyhood friends explored most of the area of the Upper East Side at one time or another. Their prime activity was playing stickball. "There were no factory-made bats in those days; we scrounged broom sticks wherever we could. Stickball was the sport of all boys. We played up and down the East Side. The rules changed from one area to another: the kids above 125th St. played with tennis balls, but no bounces were allowed. Below 125th St., we used the regular red rubber balls that most kids used. We used to play along the side of the Ruppert Brewery; its large flat walls were great for playing. We also played along the side of the El powerhouse at 74th St. and the East River. The only trouble there was that if you hit toward the east and the wind was strong, the ball ended up in the East River! We played whenever the weather allowed. One time, I was playing along 3rd Avenue under the El. I was running to make a catch, and I was in the middle of the street when two trolley cars approached in opposite directions. I was stuck in the middle and had to stand in the narrow space between the tracks as they passed. My mother happened to be on the street on her way to the store. She came running to make sure I was still alive. I was happy: I made the catch!

"The stickball games were the big thing in our lives until we were old enough to get into the bars along 3rd Avenue. Even then, we spent alot of time playing stickball and much money changed hands in the bars as bets were taken on the outcome of the games. We did ride the El to go places. I remember taking it both uptown to the Bronx and downtown toward Chatham Square. We sometimes hopped the turnstile when we were short of money, but we never did anything stupid or dangerous. No one ever thought about vandalism in those days, it was not even a word which you heard."

(previous page, top) This plumbing supply store on 125th Street, just off 3rd Avenue, makes an unusual suggestion for holiday gift giving.

(previous page, bottom) A massive station serves 125th Street, the major crosstown thoroughfare across upper Manhattan. The New York Central Railroad station is conveniently located two blocks to the west on Park Avenue. Parked eastward on 125th are a 1950 Chevrolet, a 1947 Dodge, and a 1940 Oldsmobile while a 1940 Pontiac, a 1951 Plymouth and a gray Depatment of Sanitation garbage truck glide eastbound.

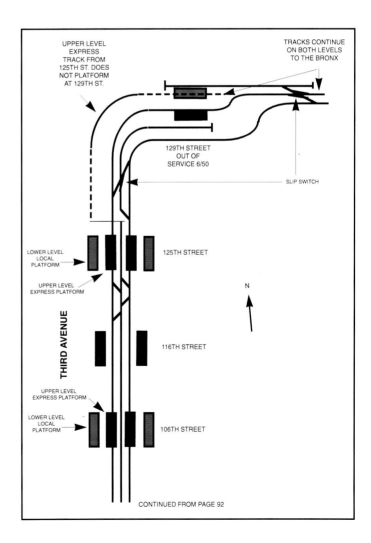

(left) A lone passenger awaits the arriving local train on the gloomy lower level southbound platform of 125th Street station.

(below) View of a man descending the stairs at 125th Street through the stain glass window. In the distance is the Manhattan entrance to the Triboro Bridge.

Recollections of Carol (born Beckhardt) Latman:

"I grew up near University Avenue in Manhattan. I went with my mother often to go shopping in the Bathgate area near 174th St. and 3rd Ave. by the El. There were lots of good buys over there. I do not remember specifically, but we must have rode the El to the antique stores and second-hand book shops near Astor Place in Manhattan. One time I discovered a 'Beckhardt Antique Store' right on 3rd Avenue under the El. Whether we were related, I never found out. The El seemed old and rickety. The space below was dark and dingy. However, once the El was gone, those same second-hand bookstores disappeared. I really miss them."

(above) In this view at 2nd Avenue and 129th St., the 3rd Avenue El structure turns northward to cross the Harlem River. The gray structure is a remnant of the 2nd Avenue El which lasted until it was demolished by 1941. The factories and warehouses in the Mott Haven area of the Bronx stand in the distance.

(left) At the Harlem River bridge, a semaphore signal beckons a train headed for the Bronx with a CLEAR BOARD aspect, i.e.: "Proceed."

(above) A day before abandonment, a work train packs up the northbound 14th Street station ticket office furniture.

NOTICE TO PASSENGERS

After 6 P. M. on Thursday, May 12, 1955, service on the Third Avenue elevated, south of the 149th Street station, will be discontinued permanently.

Free access is provided at the 149th Street station for passengers desiring to transfer from the remaining portion of the elevated line to the East and West side subways, or from the subways to the elevated.

Service on the subways has been improved to accommodate additional passengers.

NEW YORK CITY TRANSIT AUTHORITY

(left) The official abandonment notice posted in the cars shortly before the end.

THE END

So the El had to go. After 1949, ridership on public transit slumped nationwide, and this soon developed into a precipitous and steady decline through the 1950's as more people used automobiles for their means of transportation. Ridership fell in transit oriented New York City as well, although not as drastically. In 1951, voters approved a bond issue to build a four track subway under 2nd Avenue. However, the authorities diverted the money to other projects in the transit system. In April 1952, the NYC Board of Transportation curtailed service on the 3rd Avenue El south of 149th Street in the Bronx. Henceforth, trains ran from 7:30 AM to 6 PM,

<u>weekdays only</u>. Often times Lothar Stelter would catch the last downtown train in order to ride and photograph the last trip uptown.

In the Spring of 1954, the newly formed New York City Transit Authority (which superseded the Board of Transportation) issued a report which concluded the 3rd Avenue line south of 149th Street was no longer needed. The parallel Lexington Avenue Subway and bus routes purportedly had adequate capacity to carry former 3rd Avenue patrons in Manhattan. Therefore, in the best interests of the City, the El was to be closed and demolished. Operating and maintenance expenses would be saved, and property values would increase. Some public figures questioned the efficacy of obliterating a transit facility without sufficient (and promised) replacement. In 1954, the 3rd Avenue El carried over 25,000,000 riders despite its truncation and abbreviated hours of operation; in 1946 it had carried more than 86,000,000. Transport Workers Union boss Mike Quill denounced the demolition plan at a "Save-the El" rally in April 1955 as a "businessman's swindle." Some lawmakers attempted to legislate the maintenance of service through February 1956 and a guarantee that subway construction would start. All to no avail.

On Thursday, May 12, 1955, the last uptown train departed Chatham Square terminal soon after 6 PM. Lothar Stelter and his wife Josephine were on that train along with 600 others. As the photographer recalls: "We met after work at 47th Street station and waited for the train with a special sign which said this would be the last run. A policeman came through the six car train and cut the [emergency brake] rip-cords so as to prevent someone from stopping the train en route. As the train headed northward, people, whole families, came out of bars and shops, and drinks in hand toasted and waved the El good-bye."

The El stood abandoned until August 1955 when demolition began. Just before the wrecking began, a "Good-bye-to-the-El" parade was staged on 3rd Avenue. First the stations were dismantled, then the girders and bents. Finally the pillars were yanked from their foundations, and the El was gone. Some of the scrap from the El was recycled for the third tube of the Lincoln Tunnel between Manhattan and New Jersey then under construction. By February 1956, the demolition was completed. The ensuing $1,200,000 reconstruction project widenend the roadway to 70 feet and planted over 1,000 London Plane trees. There was talk of renaming the thoroughfare "Cooper Avenue" or "The Bowerie." Manhattan Borough President Hulan Jack characterized the new 3rd Avenue "a model city highway."

The cars that ran in Manhattan El service continued operating in the Bronx briefly and were soon replaced by old subway stock. During the summer of 1955, the NYCTA started scrapping the El rolling stock. The cars had their trucks and running gear removed at the 239th Street yard in the north Bronx and were then hauled by flatbed truck to an open area near the Bronx River and 174th Street. There, they were doused with fuel and burned. The cars had been fireproofed so well that the contractor had to fill the doomed cars with debris from demolished buildings in order to get the flame heat temperature high enough. The surviving steel skeletons were then cut up for scrap. The last known Manhattan-El type car ran in a work train in December 1956. None of the cars that comprised the mainstay of the 3rd Avenue El fleet in later years were preserved. The Shoreline Trolley Museum, in East Haven, CT preserved 1878 trailer "G" which made a brief return visit to 3rd Avenue as a display during the Summer of 1986. None of the stations, ironwork and stained glass were known to have been conserved in any comprehensive manner.

The few relics lie in the collections of the odd souvenir hunter. And besides, who in the 1950's cared for such *old* "outdated" (as *The New York Times* described it) stuff?

"Finis" at Gun Hill Road station along White Plains Road in the Bronx.
(Thursday, May 12, 1955)
The last train has just completed the final run.

Demolition of the 89th Street station and the new traffic light is already in place. The toddler in the stroller will not remember the El. The photographer felt very melancholic at this location. So many times he recorded the scene from the El station which disappeared little by little, day by day.

Directing the demolition.

Setting up the hoses which
feed the tools of destruction.

"Doomed Victorian ironwork."

(below) South from 83rd Street in the Autumn of 1955; only the pillars remain. Note the parked northbound 1951 Studebaker [company slogan: "First by far with a truly post-war car!"] and the Studebaker pick-up truck. Parked southward are a 1950 Pontiac and a 1947 Chrysler.

Surprise! Quick, grab the camera! El car #1705 on a flat bed truck passes the photographer's home on Nereid Avenue, in the Bronx, during the Summer of 1955. It is on its way to oblivion......

(**previous page, top and above**) Rolling stock inferno....Near the Bronx River and East 174th Street in the Bronx.

"SALUDADE"

- Portuguese for the heartfelt longing for the glories of the past.

LOST

From a strictly practical perspective, New York lost a functioning, albeit timeworn, public transit facility which was in need of rehabilitation when it destroyed the 3rd Avenue El. All of the 600 employed on the El were reassigned to other positions in the transit system. Those who reside or work in the post-1955 developments must use the perennially overcrowded Lexington Avenue Subway, the only rapid transit running the length of the east side of Manhattan. The City eventually started building a subway under 2nd Avenue; ground was broken for a two track line in 1972. Construction abruptly halted in 1975 with the City's fiscal crisis. The Transit Authority has since had to maintain three separate, completed tunnel segments. Reviving the project has been inferred in recent MTA Capital Plans and another study of transit needs of the east side of Manhattan began in early 1995. [Ironically, one of the alternatives under consideration is a concrete viaduct!] Perhaps part of it may come to fruition in the next century.

The old 3rd Avenue is gone. The pawn brokers, antique shops, the bars, cigar stores, newsstands...and the El. Generations have passed; and the memories, fond memories of that special place and its atmosphere, persist. Recorded here, because they are irreplaceable; those human adventures, all by the El.

CHAPTER THREE: EPILOG

Third Avenue Blossoms As El Disappears

> Headline in *The New York Times*
> Real Estate Section February 7, 1956

Third Avenue changed and kept on changing after 1956. New real estate development in the form of high-rise apartment towers and office buildings has flourished along Third Avenue between 7th and 96th Streets through the present day. Following the building booms from the 1960's to the 1980's, 3rd Avenue in Midtown Manhattan became an almost two mile long corridor of new high-rise office towers. When the Socony-Mobil Oil Company opened their new headquarters in late 1955 at 150 East 42nd Street, executives recounted how they demanded from the City that the El be closed before construction on their building was completed. In 1957, one developer reportedly sold off properties elsewhere in the city in order to concentrate on new projects along 3rd Avenue. In July 1960, 3rd Avenue traffic above 24th Street became one way northbound. Below 24th Street and the Bowery have remained two way.

In contrast, the Bowery and Third Avenue north of 96th Street have witnessed little, if any, private development since 1956. The streetscapes in those areas are almost unchanged since the deletion of the El. The 3rd Avenue El in the Bronx survived until April 1973 when it too succumbed to the "remove-the-blighting-El-and-improve-the-neighborhood" cant. Those neighborhoods were soon engulfed in the mid-1970's tidal wave of arson and abandonment which reduced much of the South Bronx to rubble. By the early 1980's, the El-less 3rd Avenue in the Bronx had become a way of ruins and vacant lots.

LINK

The El was a link to New York's past as the cable car has remained a link for San Francisco's. The city-by-the-bay rebuilt its 1973 cable-powered cars in the 1980's. In the 1970's, Chicago considered demolishing the 1892 elevated line that runs in its downtown area (the "loop"). However, the Windy City saw the importance of the El to the city's well-being and in the 1990's embarked on a major overhaul of its older lines. Some of the original stations, though not as ornate as New York's were, will be restored.

REMNANTS

Aside from the pillar foundations embedded in the roadway, few physical pieces of the 3rd Avenue El remain.

- Substation #5 at Division and Allen Streets still sports its MANHATTAN RAILWAY letters. Hardly anyone in the newly expanded Chinatown can recall (or imagine) the 2nd Avenue El once passed by. The building served the 3rd Avenue El through 1955.

- Substation #6 is now the 34th Street Theater playhouse.

- The 74th Street Powerhouse still stands on the East River.

- Substation #7 at 99th Street remains a Transit Authority property. Repair of turnstiles had been its reincarnation. A retaining wall from the 99th Street Yard will continue to shore the adjoining housing project far into the future.

- Substation #8 at 161st Street in the Bronx also displays its MANHATTAN RAILWAY title. The Transit Authority used it as a substation until 1977 and later sold the property. In early 1995, it was an automobile glass establishment. [When I passed on the bus, 7/31/95, the signs for the auto glass shop were painted over.]

- Some of the abutments survive near the west side of the Fordham University campus and the old 198th Street-Bronx Park terminal.

- The lower level of the Gun Hill Road station of the White Plains Road line is the only extant 3rd Avenue El station. The Transit Authority removed the tracks in the early 1980's, yet the platform remains.

Rumors have persisted that the 89th Street stationhouse was preserved by the Museum of the City of New York. No station has surfaced [no pun intended]. The Museum of the City of New York reportedly salvaged parts of the 84th Street station. Another proposal was to re-erect one of the stationhouses in Central Park. Lothar Stelter collected some signs and a stained glass panel as did a few others. In the 1950's, historic preservation had not the appreciation or constituency it has attained in recent years. Old things were to be disposed of and not saved. In 1953 someone suggested extending the new New York Thruway down Third Avenue atop the El structure! Use the El for parking was another suggestion. Different era, different outlook, different priorities.

A TRIP UP TODAY'S THIRD AVENUE

Chatham Square, Chinatown

All photos in this section were taken by the author with Kodachrome 64 film.

South on Park Row from Chatham Square

Looking north on the
Bowery from Canal Street

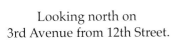

Looking north on
3rd Avenue from 12th Street.

Looking south on
3rd Avenue from 23rd Street.

Looking south on 3rd Avenue from 42nd Street

Looking north on 3rd Avenue from 42nd Street.

Looking north on
3rd Avenue from 52nd Street.

Looking north
on 3rd Avenue
from 59th St..

In the early 1990's, 3rd Avenue north of 60th Street has become a decidedly upscale shopping street as the outlets of large and trendy name-brand chain stores arrive. Meanwhile, the small shops and similar fixtures from the days of the EL diminish and disappear.

Looking north on 3rd Avenue
from 72nd Street.

Looking north on 3rd Avenue
from 88th Street.

Looking south on 3rd Avenue
from 104th Street.

Looking south on 3rd Avenue
from 128th Street pedestrian
overpass.

BIBLIOGRAPHY OF BOOKS AND ARTICLES ABOUT THE EL...

BOOKS

Cohen, Barbara; Chwast, Seymour and Heller, Stephen, eds. New York Observed, Artists and Writers Look at the City. New York: Harry N. Abrams Inc., 1987.

Cunningham, Joe, 2nd Avenue El in Manhattan. Hicksville NY: NJ International, 1995.

Cunningham, Joseph and DeHart, Leonard, A History of the New York Subway System / Part 1-Manhattan Elevateds and the IRT. Privately published by the authors, 1976.

ERA staff, Electric Railroads - All-time Equipment Roster-Manhattan Elevated. New York: Electric Railroaders Association, 1956.

Hayes, Helen with Dody, Sanford, On Reflection, An Autobiography. New York: M. Evans & Company Inc., 1968.

Kahn , Alan Paul and May, Jack, The Tracks of New York. New York: Electric Railroaders Association, 1977.

Liebman, William S., ed., Manhattan Observed. Greenwich, CT: New York Graphic Society, 1968.

Marshall, Francis, An Englishman in New York. London: G.B. Publications Ltd., 1949.

McCausland, Elizabeth, New York in the Thirties [formerly titled: Changing New York] Photographs by Bernice Abbott. New York: Dover Publications Inc., 1973.

Reeves, William Fullerton, First Elevated Railroads in the Manhattan and the Bronx of the City of New York. New York: New York Historical Society {Limited Edition}, 1936.

Rothstein, Elisia M., ed., The Artist & The El. New York: Mary Ryan Gallery, 1982.

Walker, James Blaine, Fifty Years of Rapid Transit. New York: Doubleday & Company, 1918.

Westerbrook, Dr. Wayne W., ed., and Rigby, Jim, Blizzard! The Great Storm of '88. Vernon CT: VeRo Publishing Co., 1987.

MAGAZINE ARTICLES

"Manhattan's Third Avenue," Sam Boal, *Holiday*, May 1955, pp54-60, 72-73 & 75.

"The El Comes Down," John Pile, *Industrial Design*, April 1955, pp24-31.

"Analysis of Demolishing New York City Elevated Transit Lines," Lawrence Stelter, *Municipal Engineers Journal* / Paper No. 452, LXXXVIII-Issue II, 1990, pp21-47.

"Third Avenue 'L' Track Maps," Bernard Linder, *Electric Railroaders Association/New York Division Bulletin*, March 1993.

"Third Avenue Elevated Manhattan Service Ended 40 Years Ago." *Electric Railroaders Association/New York Division Bulletin*, May 1995.

"New York's El Lines 1867-1955," *Electric Railroads* #25, ERA staff, George E. Horn, editor, December 1956.

FILMS which feature the El:

The Lost Weekend, starring Ray Milland and Jane Wyman. Directed by Billy Wilder. Paramount Pictures, 1945.

Naked City, starring Barry Fitzgerald, Howard Duff and Dorothy Hart. Directed by Jules Dassin. Universal Studios, 1948.

"Sometimes on nights like this I can still hear it rumble by."

This cartoon by Charles Addams appeared in the May 27, 1939 issue of *The New Yorker* magazine. Demolition of the 6th Avenue Elevated line has been completed a month before, and yet for some its removal evoked a melancholic sense of loss. Doubtless many on 3rd Avenue felt the same sixteen years later and into the future.